D0699677

WITHDRAWN
UTSA LIBRARIES

The traditional (monetary) approach to central banks is to consider them as monopoly institutions independent of the elected government and passive agents of money holders. Any competition among central banks in a monetary union is thought to result in an over issue problem, which has its roots in the view that moneys produced by competitive central banks are perfect substitutes for each other. In the conventional set-up over issue can be overcome by granting a central bank exclusive rights to conduct monetary policy.

In this book Mark Toma explores the workings of the early Federal Reserve System as a basis for challenging the conventional wisdom. His approach is framed in the spirit of the public choice tradition, but is novel insofar as its focus is the microeconomics of the central banking industry. He develops a series of micro-based models of the banking sector which are used to explain historical developments in central banking and in the behavior of the monetary policy makers.

Professor Toma is able to show that competition among reserve banks in the 1920s did not result in an over issue of Fed money. Rather the main effect of the competitive structure was to cause reserve banks to make substantial interest payments to the private banking system in place of transfers to the US government. He argues that the Congress imposed a more monopolistic structure on the Fed in the mid 1930s in order to accommodate the increased revenue demands of the Treasury at the time. The book is unique in emphasizing the evolution of the Federal Reserve from a competitive to a monopolistic structure.

Competition and monopoly in the Federal Reserve System, 1914–1951

Studies in Monetary and Financial History

Editors: Michael Bordo and Forrest Capie

Competition and monopoly in the Federal Reserve System, 1914–1951

A microeconomics approach to monetary history

MARK TOMA

University of Kentucky

CAMBRIDGE
UNIVERSITY PRESS

PUBLISHED BY THE PRESS SYNDICATE OF THE UNIVERSITY OF CAMBRIDGE
The Pitt Building, Trumpington Street, Cambridge CB2 1RP, United Kingdom

CAMBRIDGE UNIVERSITY PRESS
The Edinburgh Building, Cambridge CB2 2RU, United Kingdom
40 West 20th Steet, New York, NY 10011-4211, USA
10 Stamford Road, Oakleigh, Melbourne, 3166 Australia

© Mark Toma 1997

This book is in copyright. Subject to statutory exception
and to the provisions of relevant collective licensing agreements,
no reproduction of any part may take place without
the written permission of Cambridge University Press.

First published 1997

Printed in Great Britain at the University Press, Cambridge

Typeset in Monotype Times New Roman 10/12 pt

*A catalogue record for this book is available from
the British Library*

Library of Congress cataloguing in publication data

Toma, Mark.
    Competition and monopoly in the Federal Reserve System, 1914–1951:
a microeconomics approach to monetary hsitory / Mark Toma.
        p.   cm.
    Includes bibliographical references and index.
    ISBN 0-521-56258-9 (hardcover)
    1. Federal Reserve banks – History.   2. Monetary policy – United
States – History – 20th century.   I. Title.
    HG2563.T63   1997
    332.1'1'0973–dc20   96–36771
                                                                 CIP

ISBN 0 521 56258 9 hardback

Library
University of Texas
at San Antonio

To Mattie Sue

Contents

Figures

Tables

Preface

This book is a study of the Federal Reserve System that is motivated by what I perceive to be an important omission in most theoretical and applied approaches to monetary economics. Modern monetary economics has been first and foremost a demand-side theory. Whether the model of the monetary economy has been based on a static, single period assumption, an overlapping generations assumption, or an infinitely lived representative agent assumption, the emphasis has generally been on refining the theory of money demand. Many of the insights of the modern approach have been grounded in the marginal utility analysis of microeconomics.

The theme of this book is that a microfoundation of money supply is the missing element in modern monetary economics. I ask the monetary theorist to reflect on the truly bizarre nature of the modern approach to the supply side. Typical supply-side assumptions are of the genre of Friedman's famous helicopter money. Sometimes the money supplier is figuratively a helicopter, sometimes an unconstrained monetary dictator, and sometimes a central banker with a particular money supply preference (for example, a conservative central banker). The common thread to all of these assumptions is that supply tends to be exogenous. To be sure modest attempts have been made to introduce supply-side microfoundations into these models. But nowhere do we have an approach grounded in the microeconomics of supply that compares with the sophisticated treatment of demand. Such an approach would be very much in the spirit of industrial organization theory where concepts like competition among suppliers, cost of production, and industry structure play fundamental roles.

Because my background is as an applied macro economist, this book illustrates the supply-side approach by way of a particular historical example – the evolution of the Federal Reserve System up to 1951. I shall admit my bias up front and without apology. I tend to see competitive pressures everywhere and the search for these pressures represents the overriding motif of my interpretation of the Federal Reserve period. If nothing else, this search has much to offer as a counterweight to the prevailing orthodoxy which tends to cast every Fed policy as a byproduct of a discretionary Fed decision maker or else as a byproduct of a Fed reaction function which relies on numerous *ad hoc* explanatory variables. Ultimately, my approach will have to be judged by the standards applied to any economic analysis: Is it consistent with the evidence and does it further our understanding of human actions, in this case, within the realm of monetary institutions?

I would like to thank Michael Bordo for encouraging me to undertake this project. Michael's credentials as an economist who uses the latest advances in theoretical monetary economics to provide deep insights into events in monetary history are well known. What is most impressive, however, is the public goods nature of his professional activities. His feedback on my work (no matter how unorthodox my hypothesis) has often provided the basis for a fresh look at the issue at hand and always has improved the final product.

While much of the work in this book represents my latest thinking and therefore has not been previously published, some of the chapters do rely on previously published work. I thank the *Journal of Monetary Economics* for allowing me to draw from Toma (1985; 1991a), the *Journal of Money, Credit, and Banking* for allowing me to draw from Holland and Toma (1991), *Explorations in Economic History* for allowing me to draw from Toma (1989), and *The Journal of Economic History* for allowing me to draw from Toma (1992). I also thank the Earhart foundation for financial support.

1 Introduction

1.1 A microeconomics parable

Imagine that you have just received the latest textbook in advanced micro-economics theory. Flipping through you come to chapter 3, "The Theory of Markets." The first section is "Demand theory." Treating pancakes as output, the section derives a market demand function for pancakes.

In this model pancakes are special. First, they are indestructible. Second, they serve as tickets that will determine the holders' station in an afterlife. If there is only one pancake outstanding, then the holder of that pancake will assume the highest possible station. All others in the individual's age cohort will disappear into nothingness upon death. If there are two pancakes available to the cohort, then the holders of each will assume the second highest possible station in afterlife (and so on). If the amount of pancakes equals the cohort population, then everyone in the cohort has a pancake and they confer no special status. Individuals assign pancake values according to their assessment of the station pancakes will enable them to attain.

Although this theory of demand seems somewhat peculiar, you continue to the next section expecting to find a theory of supply. Instead, the title is "The problem of a determinate price level." Here you discover that pancake consumers have a problem. How can they establish their current demand without knowing the current supply and whether this supply will be aug-mented in the future? The upshot is that today's equilibrium price of pan-cakes depends on current and *all* future supplies. So the problem of a determinate price level is fundamentally an issue of whether consumers are able to look into the future and ascertain pancake supplies. If not, the price of pancakes is indeterminate.

The solution turns out to be surprisingly simple: spaceship pancakes. A spaceship appears from some unknown part of the universe and drops pan-cakes. The drop is accompanied by a (credible) voice indicating that the ship will return periodically and drop pancakes so as to keep constant the propor-tion of pancakes per cohort size. Because it enables consumers to ascertain pancake supplies in every period, this announcement is sufficient to establish equilibrium.

The next section is "Extensions of the theory." The spaceship tires of returning and designates an earthling as the pancake authority. The spaceship leaves the recipe for creating pancakes – simply fry them up (at zero resource cost) – and instructs the authority to continue with the original supply plan.

Left to herself, the pancake authority disobeys orders and announces a policy change. Instead of giving them away, she will charge for the pancakes. Also, there will be a new supply plan. A pancake economist in the community notes that the new plan is cleverly designed to maximize the present value of revenue from pancake sales.

The final section of the chapter is "The profit incentive problem." The problem is that pancakes are easy to produce (simply fry them up). The pancake authority soon finds that others are invading her turf and producing pancakes that are replicas of her own. Counterfeiters have an incentive to enter the market until everyone has a pancake. At this point, pancakes are worthless. Competition has driven the value of the total pancake supply to zero.

The section concludes by pointing out that the solution to the profit incentive problem is straightforward. The spaceship will return and reassert control. By restricting supply, perhaps by re-imposing the original distribution plan, the spaceship makes the pancakes valuable.

1.2 Modern monetary theory

Substitute "money" for "pancakes" and the microeconomics parable aptly characterizes modern monetary theory. The money market of modern theory is plagued by problems of a determinate equilibrium. The solutions offered by monetary theorists are analogous to the solutions offered in the parable. The easiest solution is to assume Milton Friedman's famous helicopter money. A more sophisticated solution is to assume a monetary authority, such as a conservative central banker (see Rogoff, 1985), with well-defined plans for the money supply. These solutions are no more satisfactory than the ones offered in the parable. They all anchor the public's expectations by introducing a supply factor from outside the model.

At a very general level, the intent of this book is to offer a solution to the problem of a determinate money market equilibrium that relies on the standard microeconomics theory of supply rather than the story line of the parable. My quarrel is not just that the spaceship assumption involves too much "hand-waving." More fundamentally, I shall argue that the analysis in the parable is not good economics. It is based on a faulty concept of competition. In the parable, as well as in modern monetary theory, competition among producers takes one form only – an increase in production. There is no recognition of the possibility that a producer may be able to preserve the value of own output by producing a differentiable product and limiting its nominal supply.

One way of introducing product differentiation into the parable is to allow a producer's output to confer a station in afterlife that is independent of the other producers' supply decisions. For instance, assume that the spaceship designated numerous monetary authorities and gave each a secret recipe for producing pancakes of a particular color. Competition in this setting would result in a commitment by each producer to make one pancake; each member of the community would hold a unique-colored pancake and each of the pancakes would confer entry into the highest station in afterlife. If a producer attempted to expand production, then its client would switch to another supplier in waiting.

What would be the market price of a pancake? Because pancakes cost nothing to produce, competition would reduce the price to approximately zero. Alternatively, producers could charge a price equal to the value of a pancake and then rebate this value to the consumer in the form of a monetary or an in-kind payment. The important point is that competition has standard optimality properties. In equilibrium, marginal cost equals marginal value and total net value is maximized.

1.3 Evolution of the economic approach to the Federal Reserve

This book focuses on the operation of a particular money supply institution – the Federal Reserve System – to illustrate the microeconomics approach to monetary theory. In the early days of the Federal Reserve, economists frequently viewed it as a public-interested organization whose primary purpose was to achieve some macroeconomic objective such as price stability. The post World War II record of persistent inflation tended to reject price stability as a predictive hypothesis. Mainstream economists then turned to income stabilization as the Fed policy objective. The System was viewed as a body of information-gathering technocrats who provided a monetary boost to the economy during recessions and exercised restraint during expansions.

Because inappropriate techniques may interfere with the Fed's ability to stabilize the economy, even a technocratic public-interested Fed was subject to advice and criticism from the academic community. Much of macroeconomics policy analysis has been directed toward providing the Fed decision maker with more refined tools for conducting stabilization policy. The most thought-provoking counsel, however, emanated from the monetarist camp. Given informational limitations, the Fed's attempt to stabilize the economy may actually be destabilizing. Since the problem was not one of motivation or improper incentives, the monetarist critique did not fundamentally change the way the macro economist viewed Federal Reserve policy making. After all, the economist could still hope to develop new and improved monetary policy techniques that might overcome the information problems.

Two independent lines of economic research in the early 1960s provided a more fundamental challenge to the public interest view. On the one hand, James Buchanan and Gordon Tullock (1962) pioneered work in public choice theory. Political decision makers were not viewed as split personalities who pursued private concerns in the market place and so-called public concerns in the political arena. Instead, the public choice approach hypothesized that political decision makers act like their private counterparts in maximizing utility subject to constraints. An important research agenda for the public choice theorist was to identify the constraints confronting policy makers. This identification process must play a fundamental role in any theory of the Fed, such as the one developed in this book, which claims a microeconomics foundation.

At about the same time as the emergence of public choice theory, the theory of rational expectations revolutionized macroeconomics. The Lucas policy-ineffectiveness critique posed a challenge to the monetarist view that Fed officials were motivated to stabilize income. If stabilization policy was not effective, then why would rational Fed decision makers attempt to stabilize? The time and effort used in a futile effort to achieve the impossible could be used to increase consumption or leisure.

Although seemingly unrelated, the public choice and rational expectations theories point to a new way of viewing Fed decision making. While rational expectations theory emphasizes the inability of policy makers to fine tune the economy, the public choice approach emphasizes that policy makers do not necessarily have an incentive to pursue a fine-tuning strategy. Work by public choice theorists on the political process in general suggests that, instead of being motivated by welfare considerations, many government programs simply redistribute wealth from one interest group to another. Furthermore, government programs generally require a revenue source. This suggests that money creation may be viewed as a means of raising revenue for funding general government expenditures.

Interestingly, the new classical, rational expectations theory reached much the same conclusion but from a different direction. Given that money creation does not have systematic real effects, the new classical approach raises the question of what drives the money-supply process. One answer is that even a welfare-maximizing government might use money as a revenue device. In a world where other revenue instruments impose deadweight losses on the general taxpayer, optimal fiscal policy considerations suggest that the government would want to raise some revenue through the inflation tax.[1]

Neither the new classical nor the public choice approaches provide a completely satisfactory basis for explaining the actions of central bankers. The problem with the new classical approach is that it tends to view the government as a black box where optimal policies automatically emerge. A typical assumption is that the government is a monolithic policy maker who passively maximizes the utility of a population of identical taxpayers. This approach ignores critical microeconomics issues such as possible principal-agent problems between the taxpayer and the appointed political representative or the politician and the bureaucrat who ultimately implements policy.

By taking institutions seriously, public choice theory brings to the forefront the issue of how taxpayers (or at least coalitions of taxpayers) design the rules of the monetary game to obtain what is in their long-run interest. But often the public choice theorist ignores the insights offered by the new classical approach about the impact of various policy rules on individual decision making. Because the way rules influence incentives depends on the connection between policy actions and the economy, and even more importantly on how policy makers and the public perceive these connections, the new classical approach to macroeconomics becomes a necessary complement to public choice theory. Specifically, the new classical approach asks the public choice theorist to consider the possibility that the policy makers' inability to manipulate real variables, like real output or real interest rates, severely restricts the set of feasible policy options.

Recent research in new classical economics (see Plosser, 1990) suggests one narrow avenue through which Fed policy can affect the real economy. Certain Fed regulations may interfere with the smooth functioning of the banking system. An important example would be the imposition of reserve requirements behind bank deposits. Reserve requirements increase the cost of banking and thereby decrease the ability of banks to transform deposits into loans. To the extent the private sector relies on loans to finance investment, reserve requirements tend to depress real output in the economy. Thus, Fed regulations such as reserve requirements represent "real" factors which can have both financial stability and economy-wide output effects.

1.4 Towards a microeconomics theory of the Federal Reserve

The public choice insight that the Fed's money creation is valued as a source of general government funding along with the new classical insight that only certain narrowly defined Fed policies affect the real economy, represent the starting point for a microeconomics theory of the Federal Reserve. Consider a monetary sector consisting of a network of competitive private clearinghouses (reserve banks) that provide liquidity for retail banks. The government can raise revenue for itself by imposing monopolistic restrictions on the reserve industry. For example, the government could grant monopoly status to a clearinghouse and then tax its profits. One consequence is that the amount of liquidity offered to the banking system would be reduced. The greater the government's financing needs the less liquidity supplied by the reserve industry and the greater the fragility of the banking system. This tradeoff between revenue needs and financial stability was at the heart of the congressional debate preceding the founding of the Fed.

Chapter 2, "The microeconomics of the reserve industry," provides the conceptual framework underlying the revenue-stability tradeoff. The chapter begins by developing a general theory of equilibrium in the private clearinghouse industry. The primary function of a clearinghouse is to provide liquidity to the banking system by guaranteeing that bank deposits at clearinghouses can be instantly converted into specie. This requires that the clearinghouses hold specie which raises the cost of providing liquidity.

The next step is to introduce a tax on clearinghouses and show how it affects equilibrium. The higher the tax, the more funds for the government but less liquidity for the banking system. The general conclusion is that there is an inverse relationship between funding needs and financial stability.

Chapter 3 considers the "Peculiar economics of the founding of the Fed." In the nineteenth century, central banks were created in response to increases in the financing requirements of national governments (see Giannini, 1995). The Act establishing the Federal Reserve System was peculiar in that it contained provisions which imposed tight constraints on the ability of the new Federal Reserve banks to generate profits. Tight constraints made sense only if current and prospective government seigniorage requirements were low. The chapter argues that such was the case when the Federal Reserve Act was debated and enacted. Introduction of the federal income tax in 1913 boosted the potential revenue from traditional sources thereby creating the expectation that seigniorage would become a less important factor in government financing. Of course, the United States participation in World War I soon after the Federal Reserve banks opened for business led to a change in expectations. A series of amendments to the Federal Reserve Act in 1917 provided reserve banks with the ability to earn profits and sizable transfers were made to the general government during the war.

Chapters 4 and 5 discuss Fed policy in the immediate aftermath of the war. The setting was unprecedented in that reserve banks were no longer shackled by the constraints of a high gold reserve nor was their policy dictated by wartime financing considerations. How would the reserve banks use their new-found freedom?

Chapter 4, "Interest on reserves and reserve smoothing in a correspondent banking system," focuses on the use of discount policy in providing an elastic money for the banking system during the 1920s. The chapter distinguishes between two types of banks – city and country banks. City banks acquire banking services from the Fed and country banks acquire banking services from the city banks. The chapter outlines the circumstances under which reserve banks would pass along some of their profits to city banks by way of implicit interest payments on reserves. City banks would also pay interest on the reserves of their country bank clientele. The result is that the overall cost to the banking system of holding reserves is lower. Perhaps of even more importance for the stability of the banking system, the seasonal fluctuation of reserve-holding costs turns out to be less pronounced with these interest payments.

Chapter 5, "Competitive open market operations," directs attention toward open market operations during the early 1920s. This was a period when profit-seeking reserve banks actively competed with each other by conducting open market operations (see Friedman and Schwartz, 1963). The consensus is that competition would cause the System to "create easy money" (D'Arista, 1994). The microeconomics view comes to the opposite conclusion. Competitive open market operations would be associated with monetary restraint and the absence of a seigniorage incentive problem. A corollary is that open market operations would lead to a scissors effect: non-borrowed reserves would displace borrowed reserves on an approximately one-for-one basis.

Chapter 6, "High tide of the Federal Reserve System?" tests the main hypotheses presented in chapters 4 and 5. Tests for the scissors effect over the decade of the 1920s show that open market operations had little effect on Federal Reserve credit. Contrary to the view offered by Friedman and Schwartz (1963), this evidence, along with evidence on seasonal movements in interest rates and Fed credit, indicates that the relative stability of the economy during the decade could not be attributed to the Fed's open market operations. The chapter concludes, however, by indicating that Fed policy may have contributed to the onset and severity of the Great Depression. By shutting down the discount window and centralizing open market operations, the Fed ended its 1920s policy of providing seasonal and emergency aid to the banking system.

Chapter 7, "The Fed, executive branch, and public finance, 1934–1939," begins with the observation that the Great Depression upset the stability of the 1920s. One effect was a surge in the government's financing requirements. To accommodate the surge, Congress passed legislation which represented the most fundamental change in the monetary sector since the founding of the Fed. Among other things, legislation established the Treasury as coproducer of money. Because Treasury money was a perfect substitute for Fed money, the government now had to be concerned about the over issue problem. The chapter argues that the solution was to make the Treasury the sole issuer of new money. This helps explain why Federal Reserve credit was constant from 1934 to 1939. The chapter also ties the doubling of reserve requirements in 1936–37 to the increase in the government's financing requirements.

Chapter 8, "World War II financing", continues the theme that structural changes in the relationship between the public and the monetary authority are brought about by shocks to the government's financing requirements. In the 1940s the government's financing requirements increased and the rate of gold inflow, which had been the basis of the Treasury's money production, decreased. The task the government faced was how to supplement the Treasury's money production without reintroducing the seigniorage incentive problem. The solution was an interest rate control program. In April 1942 the Fed agreed to support 25-year government bond prices at a level consistent with a 2.5 percent interest rate ceiling. Using a rational expectations assumption, the chapter argues that such a program required that the Fed commit to a policy consistent with low long-run expected money growth rates. To the extent that the Fed followed through on the commitment, the interest rate control program overcame the over issue problem.

The concluding chapter, "Historical lessons", briefly reviews Fed policy since World War II and suggests that the historical approach of this book offers insights into the future course of monetary policy throughout the world. Two issues seem likely to dominate the policy debate in the twenty-first century. One is the optimal constitution for a monetary union of previously independent monetary authorities and the other is the importance of central bank independence. The chapter suggests that competition may be a desirable attribute of a monetary union making the presence or absence of central bank independence largely a moot issue.

At the center of this book's account of Federal Reserve history is the government's financing requirements. Indeed, the reason that twentieth century monetary policy is interesting is due to the revenue demands the federal government has placed on the Fed. In a setting where revenue demands are insignificant the Fed can be structured to run more or less on automatic pilot. This was the situation that existed around the time of the Fed's founding. Over time there were discrete jumps in financing requirements, the most notable of which were the two wars and the Great Depression. At each of these stages, Congress passed legislation which reduced the competitiveness of the reserve industry and thereby enhanced its long-run revenue potential. Before considering the details of each stage, the next chapter will develop the basic microeconomics foundation of the reserve industry.

2 Microeconomics of the reserve industry

2.1 Overview

The traditional monetary theory of central banking has been one with little institutional detail. Operating in a closed economy, a monopoly central bank prints an initial allocation of infinitely lived, non-interest-bearing currency at a cost of zero. The central bank uses the currency to buy assets from private individuals. In subsequent periods the central bank has the option of printing new money and acquiring new assets or perhaps selling some of its previously acquired assets for old money. One of the side effects of money creation is that it provides a source of revenue equal to the nominal interest rate times the real quantity of central bank assets. This revenue is often referred to as seigniorage.[1]

Modern central banks bear little resemblance to this theoretical construct. In addition to printing money, central banks typically provide payments services (for example, check-clearing services) and lender of last resort services. They also tend to regulate the banking system, most notably, by imposing reserve requirements.

Why do modern central banks engage in such a wide range of activities? One possible explanation is that the central bank is little more than a voluntary association among private banks; that is, a banking club. According to this view, the activities of a central bank correspond to what private banks would ask from a banking club. To understand the operation of a banking club, therefore, is to understand the operation of a central bank (see Gorton and Mullineaux, 1987).

Another explanation is based on the notion that central banks do more than banking clubs. Left to themselves, banking clubs would fail to undertake certain activities that are crucial to the safety of the banking system. Backed by the enforcement powers of the state, central banks impose legal restrictions such as reserve requirements which are designed to internalize spill over effects associated with purely club activities (see Goodhart, 1987, 1988).

Kevin Dowd (1994) has argued persuasively against both of these views.

First, unlike central banks, banking clubs historically have confined themselves to strictly clearinghouse functions. So central banks are more than a replication of banking clubs. But Dowd goes on to argue against the view that central banks evolved to correct market failures. He concludes that "Recent claims to the contrary notwithstanding, banking regulation and central banking apparently did not evolve to counter inherent deficiencies in (free) financial markets. Real-world banking regulations must therefore have developed for other reasons than market failures, and the most obvious reasons are political ones. The other, complementary, conclusion is that the development of official regulations and central banking were not Pareto improvements over the free market, and cannot therefore be justified on efficiency grounds" (1994, p. 306).

This chapter provides a conceptual framework for understanding the political motivations behind banking regulation and central banking. The first step (section 2.2) is to develop a model of private reserve banks as clearinghouses. A key result is that competitive forces lead to the payment of interest on reserves which induces banks to hold more reserves than otherwise. This means that there is more liquidity in the banking system that can be drawn upon in the case of a financial emergency. After defining the competitive characteristics of the reserve market, section 2.3 introduces the possibility that the government wants to use this market to help finance a general revenue requirement. One way to do this would be to grant a reserve bank monopoly status and then tax the profits of the privileged bank. For my purposes, a state-sanctioned monopoly transforms a reserve bank into a central bank.

There is a tension between the government's revenue needs and the stability of the financial system. A larger government revenue requirement decreases the interest rate paid on reserves, decreases the amount of reserve holdings, and increases the fragility of the banking system. It was an attempt to reduce this tension that led to the founding of the Federal Reserve.

2.2 Model of reserve bank competition

The basic model of reserve bank competition starts with the assumption that there are three agents in the reserve market. In addition to reserve banks, there are retail banks (or simply banks) and the general public. Reserve banks receive deposit funds from retail banks and retail banks receive deposit funds from the general public. The only earning asset of reserve banks is loans to retail banks. The possibility that reserve banks supplement these loans with open market operations is introduced in a later chapter. With respect to the monetary liabilities of reserve banks, neither private banks nor the general public hold currency. The only liability is retail bank deposits which may pay interest.

The model also assumes that market pressures will force the reserve banks to commit to a real asset backing for their monetary liabilities at a preset conversion rate. The relative price of the real asset is determined in a worldwide market. Movements in the money price of output will be tied to movements in this relative price by the equation

$$(CR)(1/P_O) = P_G \qquad (2.1)$$

where CR is the conversion rate between units of money ($) and units of the real asset, P_O is the money price of output, and P_G is the relative price of the real asset (say gold). Setting the conversion rate at 1 gives the simple relationship $P_G = (1/P_O)$. In the absence of shocks to the real asset market, convertibility pegs the money price level.

A final set of assumptions concerns the uniqueness of reserve bank money. The reserve industry provides liquidity to the banking system by guaranteeing that the deposits retail banks hold at reserve banks can be instantly converted into the dominant money of the economy, either specie or possibly currency. Reserve banks can provide this guarantee at a cost that is lower than the cost of other guarantors in the economy. This insures a determinate demand for aggregate reserve bank money.

Given these assumptions, the first task is to derive the demand function for aggregate reserve bank money. In this set up, only banks demand reserve bank money in the form of reserves. The banks' choice problem is to choose the level of reserves that maximizes profits. Consider a version of the bank profit function used by Miron (1986) in his oft-cited work on financial panics

$$\pi_B = iS_B + rR - (w^2/2)[(R/D) - 1]^2 - dL_C, \qquad (2.2)$$

where π_B is expected real profit, i is the nominal interest rate, S_B is the planned quantity of financial assets acquired by the bank, r is the interest rate on reserves at a reserve bank, R is planned real reserves, w^2 is the variance of withdrawals, D is expected real deposits, d is the interest rate that the reserve bank sets on loans to banks, and L_C is real reserve bank loans.[2]

The primary component of bank costs is $(w^2/2)[(R/D) - 1]^2$, which reflects the liquidity costs associated with unexpected withdrawals. While the reserve bank guarantees conversion of bank deposits into the dominant money of the economy, it is not a sure source of emergency funds in the case of a shortfall of bank reserves. If a bank's reserves are inadequate because of unanticipated withdrawals, it may have to liquidate loans which imposes costs in the form of capital losses and excess brokerage fees. Expected costs rise as the variance of withdrawals rises and decline as the ratio of planned reserves to expected deposits rises. The other component of costs is the interest on discount loans from the reserve bank.

Each bank is subject to the constraint $R+S_B=D+L_C$, where, as discussed in the next section, the amount of loans extended by the reserve bank is determined by the proportion, ρ, of specie it holds to back bank deposits. A profit-maximizing bank chooses

$$R^*=D[1-(cD/w^2)], \tag{2.3}$$

where c is the bank's opportunity cost of holding a dollar at the reserve bank and is equal to $[i\rho+d(1-\rho)-r]$.

In this model two factors increase and one factor decreases the holding costs of reserves. Given the reserve bank constraint, $L_C=R(1-\rho)$, a one unit increase in R increases L_C by $(1-\rho)$ units. Therefore, one cost of holding a unit of reserves is the borrowing cost, $d(1-\rho)$. The second cost stems from the bank balance sheet which requires that if L_C rises by $(1-\rho)$ when reserves rise by 1 unit, then the bank's financial assets, S_B, must fall by ρ which entails a loss of $i\rho$. Finally, these two factors are offset by the interest payment r on reserves.

Equation (2.3) serves as the foundation of the decision problem facing reserve banks. The reserves of banks represent the monetary liabilities of the reserve bank system and hence the source of reserve bank earning assets which in this setting consists exclusively of loans to banks. The only functions of reserve banks are to clear checks and guarantee that the deposits of member banks (reserves) will be redeemed instantly into the dominant money of the economy. If specie is the only dominant money component, and if there are no substitutes for specie, then the only way a reserve bank could provide an absolute guarantee would be to back up its liabilities one-for-one with specie. More generally, reserve bank currency will be an imperfect substitute for specie. Technical substitution possibilities between specie and currency will determine a specie-liability ratio between zero and one.

The costs of reserve banks stem from the check-clearing services they provide and from explicit interest payments on bank reserves. The revenues stem from discount loans and check-clearing fees. Industry profits can be given by

$$\Pi=dL_C-rR, \tag{2.4}$$

where the interest rate on reserves, r, is a comprehensive measure that represents both explicit and implicit components. In addition to an explicit rate of r^e, the reserve bank may make an implicit payment by charging a check-clearing fee that does not cover cost. Letting f and k represent the fee and cost per unit of reserves, the interest rate on reserves is $r=r^e+(k-f)$.

Provisionally assume that reserve banks are able to form an effective cartel. The cartel's objective is to maximize equation (2.4) subject to the balance sheet constraint, $L_C + P_G G = R$ and to the minimum specie–liability ratio, $\rho = P_G G / R$, where G is specie. The constraint is based on the simplifying assumption that reserve banks normally do not exercise their power to issue currency so that neither banks nor the public hold currency. The amount of R is the decision variable of retail banks and is given by equation (2.3). Making the appropriate substitutions into (2.4) gives the cartel's maximization problem as

$$\text{Max } \Pi = D[1 - (cD/w^2)][d(1 - \rho) - r], \tag{2.5}$$

where the cartel uses d and r to control the term, $[d(1 - \rho) - r]$.

Define $z = [d(1 - \rho) - r]$ as the profit rate per unit of reserves. An increase in z has counter effects on profits. First, an increase in z increases profits per unit of reserves. Second, an increase in z increases c and therefore decreases the demand for reserves. Equating the marginal gain with the marginal loss, the cartel chooses

$$[z]^M = [(w^2/D) - i\rho]/2, \tag{2.6}$$

where the M superscript indicates the monopoly (cartel) solution. Equation (2.6) shows that a decrease in the specie ratio increases the monopoly profit rate, $[z]^M$.

Figure 2.1 illustrates the cartel solution. The cartel faces the aggregate demand curve, R, and imposes a reserve holding cost on the private banking system of $c = i\rho + z$. For a given ρ, the cartel selects a d and r combination that results in maximum profits, zR. The cartel solution at M corresponds to the point where the elasticity of demand, for the portion of the curve above the horizontal line at $i\rho$, equals minus one. The shaded area gives cartel profits.

The cartel has two techniques for implementing the cartel solution. First, it may fix a common price (that is, the d and r combination) that each reserve bank may charge. In this case private banks would be indifferent to which reserve bank supplied them with reserves. Alternatively, the cartel may forgo a pricing policy and allocate each reserve bank a market share. In this case, each reserve bank would choose its pricing policy.

Assuming homogenous reserve banks, the two techniques are equivalent. When the cartel fixes the price to generate the holding cost $[c]^M$ in figure 2.1, each private bank chooses its supplier through a flip of the coin and each of n reserve banks ends up with $[R]^M/n$ of the market. When the cartel divides the market proportionally among reserve banks, each independently chooses the common pricing policy that gives the cartel profit rate.

The reserve bank cartel, like cartels in other industries, is unstable. Each reserve bank has an incentive to expand market share by lowering the holding cost to its clientele – either by lowering the discount rate or raising

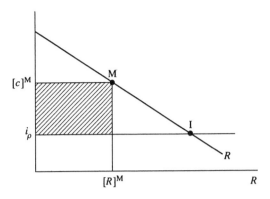

Figure 2.1 The cartel solution

the interest rate on reserves. Acting alone, a reserve bank could increase its profits by an amount equal to just less than the shaded area in figure 2.1. Since each reserve bank has an incentive to chisel, the independent adjustment solution is at I with profit rates reduced to zero. In the absence of some mechanism for detecting and punishing reserve banks which attempt to independently adjust, the competitive solution represents an equilibrium.

2.3 Legal restrictions, government financing, and banking panics

Historically, the government has served as a cartelizing agent in selected markets by passing laws which grant monopoly rights to a privileged firm. The value of these rights depends on the scope of the monopoly grant. The rights will be most valuable when a pure monopoly is offered; that is, when competition is simply banned from the market and no conditions placed on the activities of the monopoly firm. Rights become less valuable when entry barriers are relaxed or if restrictions are imposed on the monopolist.

As a starting point, consider a generic contract between the government and the privileged reserve bank that entails an unconditional lease of pure monopoly rights with the lease payment equal to a percentage of reserve bank profits. The percentage will be determined by the government's revenue needs. During periods (war) when the government's revenue requirements are high, the lease rate will be set high and during periods (peace) when the government's revenue requirements are low, the lease rate will be set low.

To formalize the contractual relationship between the government and the reserve bank, let T stand for the government revenue requirement such that

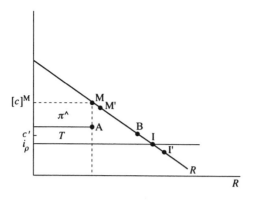

Figure 2.2 Profits tax

$$T = t(\Pi) = P, \qquad (2.7)$$

where t is the lease rate, Π is the before tax profits of the reserve bank and P is the lease payment. The objective of the privileged reserve bank under these circumstances will be to maximize profits net of the lease payment; that is,

$$\text{Max } \Pi^{\wedge} = \Pi(1-t) = D[1-(cD/w^2)][d(1-\rho)-r](1-t), \qquad (2.8)$$

which results in $c^* = [c]^M$ with the reserve bank's share of total profits, $\Pi^{\wedge}$, equal to $[z]^M[R]^M(1-t)$ and the government's share equal to $[z]^M[R]^M t$. The task of government is a straightforward one of taking the decision problem of the monopolist into account and choosing the t^* that makes $[z]^M[R]^M t = P = T$.

Point A in figure 2.2 shows the breakdown of gross profits between retained earnings, $\Pi^{\wedge}$, and an exogenous government revenue requirement, T. The figure illustrates a standard result in the public finance literature: a profit tax serves as a lump sum tax which preserves marginal conditions. As the lease rate increases or decreases with the government's revenue requirement, the distribution of profits will be affected but not the level of reserves in the banking system.

While the government covers its revenue needs at A, it does so in a way that results in a relatively low level of reserves. Reserves are low because the privileged reserve bank acts as a simple monopolist and sets a high holding cost on reserves. This has potential welfare implications because in this setup low reserves imply a low reserve-to-deposit ratio which imposes high liquidity costs, $(w^2/2)[(R/D)-1]^2$, on the banking system.

If the government is concerned about satisfying its revenue needs in a manner consistent with imposing the least cost on the banking system, then it will attempt to restructure the monopoly leasing contract in a way that forces the privileged reserve bank to lower its holding cost. For instance, instead of banning outside competition, entry rights might be extended to any reserve bank that agrees not to issue its own currency. The only way outside reserve banks could provide an absolute liquidity guarantee would be to back bank deposits one-for-one with specie; since they would not be able to pay interest on reserves, the holding cost for their retail members would be the market interest rate. The privileged reserve bank would have to do at least as good in order to attract members.

More generally, meaningful contract restructuring will occur only if outside reserve banks are able and willing to provide reserves at a cost, say c', less than $[c]^M$. The privileged reserve bank would have to reduce its holding cost accordingly and gross profits, Π, would fall. The upshot is that the government should relax legal restrictions on competing firms such that the gross profit of the privileged firm equals the government's revenue requirement. In terms of figure 2.2, the solution would be at B where by construction $\Pi = T$ and holding costs are given by the vertical distance from the horizontal axis to B. The government could capture all of these profits for itself by setting $t=1$ in the lease agreement. The privileged reserve bank earns zero economic profits and liquidity costs in the retail bank system are as low as feasible given the government's revenue requirement.

An important implication of this analysis is that there is a fundamental tension between financing needs and stability of the financial system. At one extreme, the government's requirement may be zero, making any lease agreement unnecessary. The government's job would be one of insuring position I in figure 2.2 by allowing free entry into the market. Aggregate reserves would be as high as possible and the financial system would be as safe as possible. As revenue needs rise, the government would structure a leasing contract that embodied at least some monopolistic elements. Reserves would fall and the banking system would become more prone to crisis.

Formally, the ability of the government to restructure a lease agreement implies that the choice of z is transferred from the reserve industry to the government. After setting $t=1$, the government will "choose" a z such that $zR=T=P$. Substituting $z=R/P$ and $P=T$ into the retail banking system's optimal reserve ratio, $R*/D$, and rearranging gives the implicit function

$$F=(R/D)+[T/w^2(R/D)]+(i\rho D/w^2)-1=0. \qquad (2.9)$$

Next, implicitly differentiating (R/D) with respect to T gives

$$d(R/D)/dT=-(R/D)/[w^2(R/D)^2-T]. \qquad (2.10)$$

As illustrated in figure 2.3(a), equations (2.9) and (2.10) imply a Laffer-like relationship between (R/D) and T. When $T=0$, the government chooses

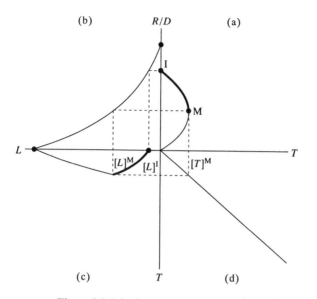

Figure 2.3 Seigniorage versus financial stability

a competitive leasing contract which from equation (2.9) results in the competitive solution, $R/D=1-(i\rho D/ w^2)$. At first, incremental increases in T reduce liquidity; that is, $d(R/D)/dT < 0$, when $T < w^2(R/D)^2$. Eventually, the point is reached, $T=w^2(R/D)^2$, where incremental increases in z no longer generate more profits and hence no longer generate more revenue for the government's financing requirements. Since liquidity and government revenue both fall, the government will never choose to increase z beyond this point. In figure 2.3(a), the relevant portion of the Laffer curve is given by the heavily shaded segment whose end points correspond to the competitive and monopoly profit rates.

While figure 2.3(a) relates financing to the reserve ratio, figure 2.3(b) relates the reserve ratio to the banking system's liquidity costs, $L=(w^2/2)[(R/D)-1]^2$. When the reserve ratio falls, liquidity is low and liquidity costs are high. According to Miron, the banking system is prone to panics during these periods of low liquidity and high costs.

Figure 2.3(c) completes the picture by indicating how a change in the government's financing requirements filters through the banking system to affect liquidity costs. For $T=0$, retail banks choose I which results in liquidity costs of $[L]^I$. For $T=w^2(R/D)^2=[T]^M$, retail banks choose M which results in liquidity costs of $[L]^M$. The general relationship between T and L is a Laffer-like one with the heavily shaded segment in figure 2.3(c) corresponding to the heavily shaded segment in figure 2.3(a). Over the relevant range, an increase in the government's financing requirements will increase the probability of banking panics.

Figure 2.3 indicates that the government can raise, at most, $[T]^M$ in revenue from the reserve banking system. What recourse does the government have if its revenue requirement exceeds the monopoly payment? A related issue is whether a government take over of the reserve industry reduces the liquidity costs associated with a particular revenue requirement. The next section addresses these issues by considering nationalization of the reserve bank industry.

2.4 Nationalization

The tradeoff between L and T in figure 2.3 is based on a private reserve bank system in which the owners have a residual claim to profits (net of the lease payment). In a model where revenue and costs are uncertain, these profits may be positive or negative. Negative profits might arise if a reserve bank faced a shortfall of reserves that forced it to liquidate assets on short notice.

The model of the reserve bank industry developed to this point, however, assumes away the possibility of reserve shortfalls. In the case where there are no substitutes for specie, a guarantee that members' deposits will be redeemed with the dominant money (specie) requires holding a 100 percent specie reserve behind deposits. In the case where "technological" conditions determine that reserve bank currency is somewhat substitutable, then the dominant money consists of both specie and currency and the guarantee requires somewhat less than a 100 percent specie reserve. The important point is that in either case a reserve bank always holds enough specie reserve to insure that a shortfall is not possible. Put differently, in a purely laissez-faire setting a reserve bank holds enough specie to insure against the possibility that its profits will be negative.[3]

The economic rationale of a government guarantee of the payments system must stem from some cost advantage *vis-à-vis* the reserve industry. One potential advantage is that, on relatively short notice, the government can call upon its tax and borrowing powers to acquire specie which may be used to accommodate the demands of retail banks to cash in their deposits at reserve banks. If these powers are sufficiently well developed, then the government will be able to guarantee the payments system with less specie reserve than if the reserve bank system were solely responsible for the guarantee. To take advantage of these powers, the government may either hold the specie in its own vaults (thus relieving the reserve bank from having to hold specie) and extract a high lease payment from the reserve bank or require the reserve bank to hold the specie (in an amount that would be lower than if the reserve bank was making the guarantee) and extract a lower lease payment.

Consider a government promise to insure the reserve bank industry against any negative profits arising from adverse interbank clearings. If a negative profit situation arises, the government will provide reserve banks with (lump sum) subsidies that return profits to zero.[4] To model the effect of this limited guarantee, assume it implies a specie ratio of ρ_g, such that $\rho_g < \rho$, and the government imposes this requirement on the reserve bank. In the system of equations (2.1–2.10), ρ_g now replaces ρ and the monopoly and competitive solutions shift to M' and I' in figure 2.2. This would generate a new set of Laffer curves (not shown) in figures 2.3(a) and 2.3(c). Liquidity costs now would be lower for any particular revenue requirement.

The central conclusion is that a government which has a cost advantage in providing liquidity to the banking system will have an incentive to effectively nationalize the interbank clearing function of reserve banks. This allows the industry to operate with lower specie backing and loosens the tension between financing requirements and liquidity costs. As a result the banking system is less susceptible to financial crisis.

2.5 Conclusion

This chapter has provided the conceptual framework for addressing what will become a key issue in the rest of the book – the evolution of the US monetary system in the late nineteenth and early twentieth centuries. For the US, identifying the driving force behind changes in monetary institutions has usually been posed as an either/or question: "Has the monetary system evolved in response to government financing requirements or to financial stability considerations?" Posing the question in this way, however, hides the interconnection between financing requirements and stability. An increase in financing requirements causes the government to restrain competition in the reserve industry in order to generate monopoly profits in which it can share. The byproduct is a retail banking sector that is more fragile and therefore more susceptible to a financial crisis. Thus, there is a tradeoff between financing requirements and stability. To the extent that the financing requirement is truly exogenous, .it represents a factor that is fundamental in explaining changes in the competitive structure of the reserve industry.

Another factor is the specie backing of money. Like financing requirements, this chapter has treated the gold reserve ratio as an element of public finance that is outside the control of the government. In particular, the specie ratio can be viewed as a "technology" variable that influences the cost of collecting seigniorage. A technical innovation (a decrease in the ratio) reduces collection costs and lessens the tension between financing requirements and stability. For a given financing requirement, the innovation allows the government to restructure the reserve industry in a way that makes it more competitive. The overriding theme, therefore, is that public finance considerations, whether in the form of changes in financing requirements or technical changes in the specie ratio, are the driving force behind the evolution of the US monetary system.

3 Peculiar economics of the founding of the Fed

> It is almost literally true that the Federal Reserve System, as originally conceived, was simply the nationalization of the private clearinghouse system.
>
> (Gorton, 1985, p. 277)

3.1 Introduction

The quote by David Gorton provides a concise, although slightly misleading, statement of the hypothesis that forms the basis of this chapter. The quote suggests that the founders of the Fed intended to create a national clearinghouse rather than a modern central bank. It is misleading, however, in that the founders did not necessarily intend full nationalization. The hypothesis to be presented in this chapter is that the Federal Reserve consisted of national clearinghouse banks that were to compete along side the private clearinghouse system.

One goal of this chapter is to provide a conceptual framework for evaluating this narrow version of the nationalization hypothesis. In so doing, it will be necessary to investigate the conditions leading to the passage of the Federal Reserve Act. The US monetary system in the nineteenth century was governed by the National Banking Act of 1864. This legislation created a new type of currency, the national bank note, with collateral backing of government bonds. The rationale was to provide a source of revenue for financing the outlays associated with the Civil War. Subsequent changes in financing conditions in the early twentieth century made the National Bank System obsolete and led to the founding of the Fed.

A peculiar aspect of the founding of the Fed has gone largely unnoticed in the modern literature. The founders created a system that in practice resulted in a 100 percent gold reserve behind the monetary liabilities of the twelve reserve banks. This led to an "earnings problem." The new system, as originally conceived and constructed, did not provide reserve banks with the opportunity to earn profits and hence did not generate seigniorage for the general government. The conclusion of this chapter is that this attribute of the new system can be explained on the basis of public finance considerations. Simply put, financing conditions leading up to the Fed's birth no longer warranted a monetary system which would provide revenue for the general government.

3.2 Nineteenth-century monetary policy

If one were to choose the event which most shaped the monetary system prior to the birth of the Fed a likely candidate would be the Civil War. The war was important for two reasons. First, it corresponded to a significant increase in overall government financing requirements. Second, the war limited the scope of international trade and therefore limited the amount of funds that could be raised in the short run from the primary tax instrument, tariffs. The upshot was a significant increase in the burden placed on borrowing (future taxes) and on money as revenue-raising devices.

Monetary institutions as they existed in the 1860s precluded such a straightforward response. Most important, the gold standard was a major obstacle to relying more heavily on money as a financing device. If currency had to be backed by gold, then there was little opportunity to increase seigniorage. In terms of the theory presented in the previous chapter, the war required greater financial resources than what could be produced by the prevailing system.

The gold standard obstacle to the financing dilemma was at least temporarily lifted in 1862 when the government and then the banks left the gold standard by suspending specie payments. Bordo and Kydland (1992) have provided a framework for understanding the general issue of suspended convertibility. They interpret suspension within the context of an implicit contract between the public and the government which states that the government may suspend convertibility and reduce the specie ratio to zero during an emergency, like war, as long as it promises to re-establish convertibility after the emergency. To the extent that the war itself is outside of the government's control, the wartime reduction in the specie ratio can be interpreted as an exogenous "technology" shock which temporarily reduces the cost of collecting seigniorage. Taken together with the temporary decrease in the non-seigniorage tax base (international trade) and the increase in revenue requirements, the temporary decrease in seigniorage collection costs called for increased seigniorage in current and future periods, but with a greater effect during the emergency.

A stylized depiction of the optimal intertemporal policy is given in figure 3.1(a). Laffer curve, L_0, represents the prewar situation when gold reserve requirements restricted the maximum amount of seigniorage that could be raised. For illustrative purposes, suppose that seigniorage requirements were zero so that point A is the prewar solution. The wartime emergency had the effect of reducing the gold reserve ratio which generated Laffer curve L_1. The government could now finance the emergency seigniorage requirement, say T_1. The result would be position B. Then, after the emergency, the gold standard would be re-imposed and the Laffer curve would return to its original position. With the restoration of international trade, seigniorage requirements would be lower than T_1. They would exceed 0, however, since the war is assumed to have a permanent effect on government expenditures. The result is a postwar solution at C, where seigniorage raised, T_2, is between 0 and T_1.

The crucial issue is whether it would have been reasonable, from the vantage point of the 1860s, to have expected that the monetary system introduced by the National Banking Act of 1864 would produce the type of intertemporal policy depicted in figure 3.1(a). The first thing to note is that the Act created a new currency, national bank notes, to supplement other types of national currency in circulation such as United States notes. The Treasury earned revenue on national bank notes because of a tax imposed on each note in circulation. Seigniorage available to the government for general funding purposes would equal the tax receipts less any revenue the Treasury would have to set aside for backing the national bank notes with specie.

During the period of suspension (1862–78) the amount set aside would be zero and all of the tax receipts from note issue would be available for general funding. With resumption in 1879 the Treasury would need to hold substantial quantities of gold to insure convertibility.[1] Given this gold backing, national bank note seigniorage would tend to go down. Thus, the basic setup of the National Banking Act would be expected to deliver the type of intertemporal policy required by the fiscal conditions of the time: from a prewar environment calling for zero seigniorage (position A in figure 3.1(a)) to a wartime emergency calling for significant seigniorage (position B), and finally to a postwar peace calling for lower, but still positive, amounts of seigniorage (position C).

3.3 The rationale for a new monetary system

While originally passed as a financing tool, the National Banking Act also had financial stability implications. One implication stems directly from the provisions in the Act making national bank note issue an important source of government finance. An increase in the tax imposed on notes issued by national banks would increase their operating costs and reduce the amount of liquidity in the banking system. Figure 3.1 shows this liquidity effect with positions A′, B′, and C′ in panel (c) corresponding to A, B, and C in panel (a). Comparing prewar positions A and A′ with postwar positions C and C′, liquidity is lower and the economy more susceptible to financial crisis after the war.

This type of liquidity problem was related to another – the absence of form-seasonal elasticity. Form-seasonal elasticity has been defined as "the ability at critical times to convert one form of money into another without

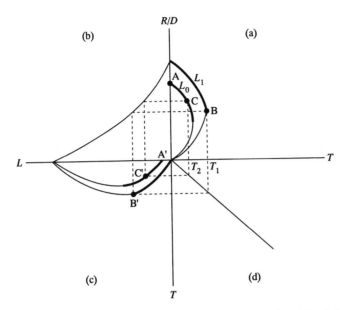

Figure 3.1 Seigniorage, liquidity, and the National Bank System

causing undue change in the total quantity of money" (Timberlake, 1993, p. 254). Because of the requirement that government bonds serve as collateral backing, notes could not readily be expanded by the banking system in response to the public's demand for currency. This posed a particular problem during an "active" season when the public was withdrawing currency from the banking system. The expected cost to running the banking system would be high and therefore the banking system would be most susceptible to a panic at this time (see Miron, 1986).

Given this seasonal liquidity problem, along with the longer-run liquidity problem caused by the high overall seigniorage requirements, the theory predicts that the period preceding creation of the Fed would be characterized by frequent financial panics. As has been well documented by a number of sources, a series of banking crises did occur during the late 1880s and early 1900s (see, for example, Sprague, 1913, chapter 3). While there is general agreement among both contemporary and modern day economists that these crises were a major motivation for the founding of the Fed, the particular method by which the Fed originally was designed to solve the financial crises problem is controversial.

One way of viewing the controversy is whether the Fed was to function as a modern central bank or as little more than a national clearinghouse. The policy debate leading up to the Fed's creation focused on the central banking responsibilities that had been undertaken by Treasury Secretary Shaw in the early 1900s. A series of budget surpluses allowed the Treasury to accumulate a substantial surplus fund. In an attempt to make currency form seasonal, Shaw used the surplus to conduct open market operations during the fall season of financial strain. The Democratic party tended to endorse Shaw's operations and wanted to institutionalize them in the form of a central bank with substantial monopoly powers. The Democrats wanted to enlarge, or at least preserve, the scope of nationalization. Their intent was that the taxing powers of the general government would underwrite any losses incurred by the central bank.

In contrast, the Republican party wanted to replace Shaw's discretionary approach with a reserve bank structure that would automatically produce form-seasonal movements in currency. According to this approach, the general government would not enlarge upon the guarantee that had been provided by the general government before 1914. Indeed, the National Bank System was to be replaced by a monetary system that was more akin to the one preceding the Civil War rather than to a modern central bank. The key innovative feature was a collection of competing government clearinghouses which would face a bottom-line and function along side the already existing private clearinghouse system.

The modern central bank and the more narrowly focused clearinghouse approaches can be evaluated on the basis of public finance considerations which predict that fundamental changes in monetary institutions are caused by shocks to the government's taxing powers and to the government's revenue requirements. The modern view of a fully nationalized central banking system would seem to be appropriate if the government's requirement for seigniorage increased. The view that the founders created a competitive reserve banking system of limited national scope would seem to be appropriate if the government's requirement for seigniorage decreased.

When the Federal Reserve Act was passed in December 1913, there were no notable changes in either government expenditures or tax revenues. The real issue, however, is whether any shocks occurred in the process of drafting the Act that would have given the founders reason to expect that expenditures and/or tax revenues would change significantly in the future. On the expenditure side, one obvious candidate is the military buildup that would accompany the US entry into World War I. But to assume that this buildup would have been foreseen by the founders of the Fed seems unlikely: the war did not breakout until June 1914 and US participation occurred much later in 1917. There is no shock that the monetary historian might point to which would lead to the conclusion that the founders could have reasonably forecast the run-up of expenditures that eventually did occur.

The situation is different with respect to the revenue side of the ledger.

The 16th amendment to the US Constitution, authorizing a federal income tax, was ratified in February 1913. At this time the income tax applied only to the richest 2 percent of the population. It was not unreasonable to forecast, however, that the tax base at some future date would be broadened. Put differently, it was not unreasonable for the founders to have expected that the taxing powers of the US would increase significantly. With the time path of expenditures expected to be unchanged and with tax revenues expected to increase, the government's seigniorage requirements would fall. This provided a rare opportunity. The founders could satisfy the (reduced) seigniorage requirements and address the form-seasonal elasticity problem by constructing a system of competitive reserve banks whose issue of currency would not be restricted by the collateral requirement of government bonds.

The case for interpreting the creation of the Federal Reserve along simple clearinghouse lines has recently been taken up by Richard Timberlake. His clearly stated position on this issue is worth quoting at length:

Creation of the Federal Reserve banks was in part a reaction to the Treasury policies that Shaw had developed. Equally important was the anticipation that the new system would promote form-seasonal elasticity in the money supply – the monetary problem publicized by many economists and politicians, and by Boutwell and Shaw at the policy level – not through the discretion of a government official, but on the initiative of commercial bankers themselves through a supercommercial (Federal Reserve) bank. The emphasis shifted from discretionary policy by a government agency to automatic and self-regulatory policy in the market. Indeed, the early Federal Reserve System, operating on a real-bills principle and on the doctrine of maintaining the discount rate above market rates of interest, was to be a self-regulating appendage to a more fundamental self-regulating system – the operational gold standard.

One can argue that Congress in fashioning the Federal Reserve System was far from single-valued about either the means or the ends of policy. However, congressmen offered no arguments that would have had the new institutions usurp the functions of the gold standard. In giving the Federal Reserve only limited powers, Congress did not feel the need to constrain the Fed's policies with explicit rules and goals.   (Timberlake, 1993, pp. 249–50)

In this view, the Federal Reserve System was intended to be a self-regulating, clearinghouse system operating on a real-bills basis. Because it represents a challenge to the modern-day consensus, this interpretation will be labeled the revisionist view.

3.4 The Federal Reserve Act: reserve banks as monopolists or competitors?

The revisionist hypothesis that a major purpose of the founders of the Federal Reserve was to replace a monopolistic currency-issuing institution, the Treasury, with a more competitive currency-issuing institution depends critically on the meaningfulness of viewing the Federal Reserve banks as clearinghouses operating in a market-like setting. At a minimum, this characterization would seem to require that reserve banks produce a well-defined output and that the decision makers at reserve banks have a claim to earnings. Then, the competitiveness of the system could be determined by identifying factors which tend to interfere with ease of entry into the reserve market as well as restricting competition among the reserve banks already in the market.

The Federal Reserve Act was the dominant factor shaping the structure of the new system. First, consider the type of output produced. Each reserve bank was to offer two types of monetary liabilities – deposits of member banks and Federal Reserve notes. Section 17 of the Act made reserve banks responsible for "servicing" these liabilities by authorizing them to act as clearinghouses in providing payments services associated with check-clearing and the handling of currency.

With respect to the earnings issue, the Federal Reserve Act nominally designated member banks as shareholders. They were required to subscribe to the capital stock of their reserve bank in an amount equal to "six per centum of the paid-up capital stock and surplus of such bank." Stock ownership, however, did not convey voting powers. Moreover, the Act gave reserve bank management first call on earnings to finance "all necessary expenses." Next, member banks were to receive a dividend payment on the paid-in capital stock. Finally, "after the aforesaid dividend claims have been fully met, all the net earnings shall be paid to the United States as a franchise tax, except that one-half of such net earnings shall be paid into a surplus fund until it shall amount to forty per centum of the paid-in capital stock of such bank." One thing the Act did not do was authorize transfer payments from the general government to the individual reserve banks in case of a shortfall in earnings. In this sense, the reserve banks faced a bottom line somewhat akin to that faced by for-profit firms in a market setting.[2]

The Act also contained provisions which affected the monopoly power of the individual reserve banks. For one thing, the Act created 12 reserve banks each operating inside a distinct geographic boundary. National banks located in a particular district were required to become members of the reserve bank in that district. Additionally, the Act granted individual reserve banks the authority

(1) "To buy and sell . . . bonds and notes of the United States, and bills, notes, revenue bonds . . . issued . . . by any State, county. . . .

(2) "To purchase from member banks and to sell . . . bills of exchange arising out of commercial transactions. . . .

(3)   "To establish from time to time, subject to review and determination of the Federal Reserve Board, rates of discount. . . ."

Nominally, each reserve bank was a regional monopolist that had the power to control its money issue, either through open market operations in government securities and bills of exchange (bankers' acceptances) or through discount loans to member banks.

The aptness of the regional monopoly label depends on the ability of individual reserve banks to coordinate their price and output decisions either through a formal cartel agency or through informal cartel-like agreements. The Act did create a central administrative unit, the Federal Reserve Board, and granted it significant price-setting powers. First, the Board could set "the charge which may be imposed for the service of clearing or collection rendered by the Federal reserve bank" (section 16). Second, the Act authorized the Board to set the buy and sell rate on open market transactions in bills of exchange (open market operations in government securities was to be at the market rate). Third, the Federal Reserve Act qualified the power of each reserve bank to establish discount rates by including the phrase "subject to review and determination of the Federal Reserve Board." At least on paper, these delegated powers established the Board as a legislatively-sanctioned body which could attempt to implement a cooperative (monopolistic) outcome on behalf of the entire system.

In practice, however, the characterization of the reserve banks as regional monopolists is misleading. A true regional monopoly would require that each reserve bank be protected from competition by firms outside the system and by other firms within the system. There must be restrictions which make entry into the market served by reserve banks prohibitively expensive. There also must be restrictions which make it unfeasible (or non-profitable) for individual reserve banks to make price and/or output decisions which would increase own demand at the expense of other reserve banks in the system. In other words, any one reserve bank must not be able to undercut the cartel by pricing its reserves at a level below the cartel-sanctioned level.

Consider first the issue of entry by outside competitors. Prior to the Fed, several types of private institutions offered payments services to the banking system. For one thing, large national banks in urban centers frequently organized private clearinghouses which would hold deposits for the national banks and supply them with check-clearing services. The large national banks in turn might form correspondent relationships with the smaller and more rural banks in their region. This would entail holding the deposits of these rural banks and supplying them with check-clearing services. Thus, private clearinghouses and large national banks, acting as correspondent banks, provided many of the same services that Federal Reserve banks were to provide.

In drafting the Federal Reserve Act, the founders made an explicit decision to retain the essential features of the correspondent banking system. In particular, the Federal Reserve Act maintained the distinction between national and state banks. While those banks choosing national charters did have to become members of the Federal Reserve System, there was no requirement that they obtain their payment services from the reserve banks. Conceivably, a reserve bank could charge such a high service fee for check-clearing, or perhaps offer check-clearing services of such poor quality, that a national bank would reject the reserve bank service and turn to the local private clearinghouse. Note, also that a bank which already had a national charter could switch to a state bank charter and these state banks had the option of signing up with the Fed or else remaining outside the Fed System. If a state bank rejected Fed membership, then it tended to rely on the national banks to supply them with payment services. The intent of the founders was unmistaken: the Federal Reserve Act confronted the reserve banks with competition from two important private sources – private clearinghouses and large national banks.

In addition to competition between the Fed and the private sector, a loophole in the Federal Reserve Act allowed for the possibility of competition among the reserve banks themselves. According to the Act, the one margin of adjustment over which individual reserve banks unambiguously could exercise discretion was the amount of government securities to buy and sell. These open market operations were to be at the initiative of the individual reserve banks and each bank was to have first claim to the earnings generated by the government securities in its portfolio.

The role of open market operations as a cartel-busting device was immediately recognized by the reserve banks. Consider a passage introducing a study prepared in 1971 by Jane D'Arista (Staff Member, House Committee on Banking and Currency) on early Federal Reserve monetary policy.

a power struggle began almost immediately after the Reserve banks opened for business in November, 1914 when the Federal Reserve Board pressured the Reserve banks for lower and more uniform discount rates and the Reserve bank Governors resisted. The Board won this round but lost the struggle. The Reserve banks won the struggle for power by dominating the System's open market operations.

(D'Arista, 1994, p. 2)

Based on this account, open market policy can be viewed as the competitive mechanism through which individual reserve banks could chisel on an attempt by the Board to use the discount rate as an instrument of coordination.

3.5 Modeling Fed policy at birth

The discussion to this point has suggested an analogy between the reserve market and the markets of microeconomics textbooks: the Federal Reserve Act created a system of 12 reserve banks each of which not only had to do battle with the competitive pressures emanating from the "external" private correspondent banking system but also with the competitive pressures "internal" to the reserve banking industry. Internally, there was an inherent tension between the collective interests and the individual interests of reserve banks. Collectively, their interests were to charge a monopoly price to demanders of reserves. Individually, each had an incentive to conduct independent open market operations at a price (reserve holding cost) that would be attractive enough to take business away from the other reserve banks in the System.

The Board was the collective agent charged with the mission of suppressing these external and internal competitive pressures. Conceivably, Board powers could be of such strength that it would be in a position to impose monopoly "prices" and "output." If, on the other hand, Board powers proved weak, then competitive "prices" and "output" would result.

When the reserve banks opened for business in 1914, however, they operated in a truly peculiar setting that dictated a policy outcome regardless of the market structure of the System; that is, regardless of the cartel power of the Board. As described by Fishe (1991), the reserve banks followed a strategy of investing all of their monetary liabilities in gold. Given this 100 percent gold reserve ratio, reserve banks would have little scope to pursue a monopolistic policy. They would have to adopt what figuratively might be referred to as a straitjacket policy, or else face the prospects of bankruptcy.

The discount model presented in chapter 2 will serve as the basis for modeling the Fed's straitjacket policy at birth. Following Fishe's lead, the key assumption is that the newly created reserve banks faced a gold reserve ratio of 100 percent. The remaining assumptions are motivated by the Federal Reserve Act which, as discussed in section 3.4, defined the Fed's market structure in rather precise terms. First, instead of a single privileged bank, the Fed consisted of a system of 12 reserve banks. Second, the reserve banks were instructed to accommodate demand in making discount loans. Third, a central administrative unit, the Federal Reserve Board, was to be in charge of setting the discount rate. Fourth, the individual reserve banks could supplement demand-determined discount loans with open market operations. Fifth, retail banks had an option of joining the Fed or joining a private clearinghouse. Sixth, member banks were required by the Federal Reserve Act to purchase stock in the System.

Incorporating these features into the basic model requires that the balance sheet of the reserve industry be reformulated. Defining S_C as the real amount of government securities held by reserve banks and E as member banks' equity holdings gives the new balance sheet constraint, $S_C + L_C = R(1 - \rho) + E$. Moreover, with $\rho = 1$ the constraint simplifies to $S_C + L_C = E$. The System could acquire earning assets, but in an amount limited by the member banks' equity. In effect, reserve banks made loans to member banks, or supplied funds through open market security purchases, and member banks returned these funds in the form of paid-in capital.

The 100 percent gold reserve ratio implied that System profits could be divided into independent components: profits from paid-in capital, Π^E, and profits from supplying reserves, Π^R. Symbolically

$$\Pi = [\Pi^E] + [\Pi^R] = [(iS_C + dL_C) - eE] + [- rR], \tag{3.1}$$

where e is the dividend rate on member bank equity. From the Federal Reserve balance sheet, $S_C = E - L_C$. Making this substitution and rearranging gives

$$\Pi = [E(i - e) - L_C(i - d)] + [- rR]. \tag{3.2}$$

The variables E, R, and L_C were not under the direct control of the Fed. The Federal Reserve Act established the equity contribution as a fixed percentage of member banks' capital and surplus. Both reserves and Fed loans were determined by member banks.

For Fed loans, the member banks' demand would depend on the relationship between the market interest rate and the discount rate. Figure 3.2 depicts this relationship in the Fed "equity market." The discount rate is plotted on the vertical axis and equity on the horizontal axis. Let i_0 be the market interest rate. If $d > i_0$, then retail banks would rely on Fed open market operations to acquire non-borrowed funds which would be used for paid-in capital. In this case, $E^B = 0$ and $E^{NB} = E$, where the B and NB superscripts designate borrowed and non-borrowed. If $d \leq i_0$, then $E^B = E$ and $E^{NB} = 0$. Retail banks would acquire funds for paid-in capital by visiting the discount window.

Because the Federal Reserve Act created the Fed as a complement to the private clearinghouse system, profits in (3.2) would be constrained by the ability of retail banks to choose membership in a private clearinghouse instead of the Fed. The private system differed from the Fed in that the clearinghouses did not have the legal power to issue currency. The only service provided was check-clearing for members. They tended to back clearing balances one-for-one with specie and charge a service fee that just covered cost.

The existence of a private clearing system as a viable option for retail banks meant that Federal Reserve banks would have to provide net benefits

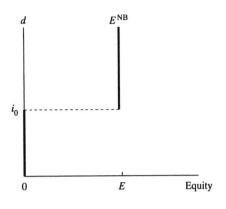

Figure 3.2 Fed equity

for members at least equal to what they would receive privately. Since reserve banks did not enjoy a cost advantage (Fed and private clearing-houses both had a 100 percent gold reserve ratio), the Fed would be subject to the same profit constraint facing private clearinghouses. Assuming a competitive private system, the Fed would be constrained by the zero profit condition $[\Pi^E]+[\Pi^R]=0$. Also, member banks initially had the option of joining the Fed and obtaining their clearing services privately.[3] This option meant that the Fed could not charge a service fee in excess of costs; that is, $r \geq 0$ which implies $[\Pi^R]=[-rR] \leq 0$. The upshot is that in order for reserve banks to survive on their own, $[\Pi^E] \geq 0$. Profits in the equity market would have to be at least zero.

Given E and the functions R and L_C, Fed profits in (3.2) would be contingent on the policy variables d, r, and e. One option was for the founders to have established precise levels for the three variables within the Federal Reserve Act. The other option was to have delegated control to the newly created Fed. The actual strategy chosen was to mandate only one of the policy variables – the dividend rate. It turns out, however, that the particular value of 6 percent chosen for e all but eliminated any effective control the Board and reserve banks might have exercised over the other variables, d and r, in the immediate aftermath of the Act.

What was special about 6 percent? This was approximately the rate on short-term assets during the period preceding the passage of the Federal Reserve Act in December of 1913. Note, for instance, that the rate on commercial paper of 4 to 6 months averaged 6.2 percent for 1913. Thus, the founders established an equity rate that was comparable with the rate on short-term assets retail banks could have acquired in the absence of an equity payment.

Returning to profit condition (3.2), if $e=i$, then $[\Pi]^E = [- L_C(i-d)]$. Since $[\Pi]^E$ was constrained to be greater than or equal to zero, an equity rate set equal to the market rate would require that the Board satisfy $d \geq i$. By establishing $e=i_0$ (where the 0 subscript now signifies the Fed's birth) in the Federal Reserve Act, the founders could anticipate that this would force the Board to reject a subsidy rate for the discount rate.

The general conclusion is that, as the Fed opened for business, the Board was in the position of a "price-taker." It had little choice but to set the interest rate on reserves equal to zero ($r_0=0$) and the discount rate equal to the market rate ($d_0=i_0$). This policy would insure that the newly created reserve banks would start off in a break-even position and at the same time close off any incentive they might have to conduct open market operations.[4]

Do the predictions of the micro model match the policy actually chosen by the Board at the birth of the Fed? With respect to discount policy, the model predicts a discount rate that equals 6 percent – the prevailing market rate of interest and the rate of return on Fed equity. With respect to interest payments on reserves, the model predicts that reserve banks would impose service charges to cover costs – significant explicit nor implicit interest payments would not be made. On both counts, the model performs reasonably well. Although there was some sentiment for a below market discount rate (see D'Arista, 1994), the Board eventually agreed to an opening rate of 6 percent.[5] The service charge policy was eclectic. At first there was no uniform, systemwide check-clearing policy as reserve banks crafted their own plans and implemented them at various times throughout 1914 and early 1915. The general tendency, however, was for reserve banks to charge service fees in an attempt to recoup costs (see Spahr, 1926, chapter VI).

A final set of predictions pertains to the magnitude and composition of reserve bank earning assets. Because member banks' reserves were backed one-for-one with gold, earning assets could only come from the equity contributions of member banks. Also, with $d=i$ member banks would tend to finance their equity contribution by borrowing from the discount window.

An examination of Federal reserve bank balance sheets in the early months of the System support these predictions. In December 1914, total gold (and lawful money) equalled $268 million which represented 100.3 percent of deposit and Federal Reserve note liabilities. The System's earning assets totalled only $11 million with discounts equal to $10 million and security holdings equal to $1 million. The $11 million in combination with $7 million of miscellaneous assets matched the Fed's equity of $18 million.

In summary, the "straitjacket" predictions of the micro model do reasonably well in explaining the set-up of the Federal Reserve System at birth.

Discount rates were tied to market and equity rates, service fees were charged, and earning assets consisted primarily of discount loans to member banks the proceeds of which were "returned" to the Fed in the form of Fed equity. As long as the specie ratio stayed around 100 percent, these straitjacket results would continue to apply. Moreover, as long as market conditions did not change appreciably, these results would represent a sustainable long-run equilibrium. For one thing, systemwide profits would be non-negative. Second, reserve banks would have no incentive to conduct open market operations; an open market operation would simply displace a discount loan without affecting profits. Finally, retail banks would find that they do no better or worse as members of the Fed compared with membership in the private clearinghouse system.

3.6 The problem of earnings

Early on, however, reserve banks found themselves confronting what was commonly referred to in the contemporary literature as an earnings problem. Henry Parker Willis, Secretary of the Federal Reserve Board from 1914 to 1918 and professor of banking at Columbia University, discussed this problem at length:

> During the first year or two of the reserve banking system, it had seemed likely that the institutions would not be able to do more than pay expenses. One or two of them had paid dividends to stockholders, but had succeeded in doing so only by counting every possible source of enhancement in value of assets, by spreading out their organisation expense over a considerable period, and by otherwise giving themselves the advantage of all doubts. As has been seen at an earlier point, it had been seriously argued by members of the Federal Reserve Board that the reserve banks if "properly run" could never pay their capital stock to the member banks. This effort had been frustrated, and it had been determined to go on as originally intended under the act with a moderate paid-up capital. (Willis, 1923, p. 1420)

It is interesting that the earnings problem was considered endemic to the System as it emerged from birth: The Board "seriously argued" that even "properly run" reserve banks "could never pay their capital stock."

According to the micro model, a long-run earnings problem indeed would arise if market conditions changed in a particular way after the Fed's birth. Suppose at $t=1$, there was a permanent fall in the interest rate such that $i_1 < d_0$. The demand for borrowed equity now would switch from E to zero in figure 3.2. The discount rate for $t=1$ would depend on whether the Board was able to adjust continuously or discontinuously.

With continuous adjustment, the Board sets $d_1 = i_1$. Reserve banks finance all of their paid-in capital from discount loans, $(E^B)_1 = E$, and earn negative economic profits in the equity market. The Board would like to either decrease e or set $r < 0$, but the Federal Reserve Act precludes these policies. The System is not in a sustainable position.

With discontinuous adjustment, $d_1 = i_0$. Reserve banks would now finance all of their paid-in capital from open market purchases, $(E^{NB})_1 = E$, and, as in the continuous case, would earn negative economic profits in $t=1$. Assuming adjustment takes place after one period, the Board would lower the discount rate in $t=2$ to $d_2 = i_1 = i_2$. Discount loans displace open market operations, but the negative economic profits persist. Therefore, whether adjustment is continuous or discontinuous, a change in conditions that permanently lowers the interest rate below the dividend rate results in a policy solution that is not sustainable.[6]

In contrast, a rise in the interest rate whether permanent or temporary need not result in a policy adjustment. If $i_1 > d_0 = e$, then $E^B = E$. Reserve banks still would be breaking even since their return from supplying funds for equity, d_0, equals the dividend rate, e. Also, retail banks would be indifferent to membership in the System. A positive shock, unlike a negative shock, to the interest rate does not pose an earnings problem.

The observation that an earnings problem emerged at the Fed's birth leads to a simple test of the micro model. A declining interest rate after 1914 provides supporting evidence while an increasing rate works against the model. The evidence is striking. Interest rates (commercial paper rates) averaged 6.2 percent and 5.4 percent in 1913 and 1914. In November 1914 the rate stood at 6.44 percent. Then it dropped to 4.88 percent in December and stayed below this level for all of 1915 and 1916, varying between 3.45 percent and 4.38 percent. This record provides clear support for the micro model's prediction that a persistent earnings problem requires as a precondition that market interest rates be persistently lower than the Fed's equity rate of 6 percent.

3.7 Financial stability

From a financial stability perspective, the main innovations of the Federal Reserve System were twofold. First, the Federal Reserve Act eliminated the government bond backing of currency. Second, the Act shifted seigniorage collection from the Treasury to the Fed and gave the Fed clearinghouse responsibilities not possessed by the Treasury under the previous system.

The importance of the first innovation is that it held the promise of a seasonal currency supply. This would tend to reduce the probability of financial crisis in the retail banking system during periods of seasonal strain. The second innovation was important because it offered an avenue through which interest could be paid on reserves. Such payments would reduce the overall cost of running the retail banking system and thereby lower the probability of financial crisis across all seasons.

As emphasized above, the peculiar economics of the Fed was that at its founding the reserve banks' monetary liabilities were backed essentially one-for-one with specie. This effectively imposed a straitjacket on the Fed, making a policy of seasonal currency supply and interest payments on reserves a moot point. The straitjacket, however, tended to be perceived as a temporary feature of the System. Once reserve banks had established a reputation of trustworthiness they might then be in a position to fulfil their commitment to convertibility with less than a 100 percent specie reserve. At this time, the Act could be amended in a way that would relax the one-for-one backing. Reserve banks would no longer have an "earnings problem" and given sufficient competitive pressures they would have an incentive to pay interest on reserves with the magnitude of these payments rising during periods of seasonal strain.

3.8 Conclusion

The public finance motivation highlighted in this chapter played a relatively minor role in the political and economic debate leading up to the founding of the Fed. Instead, the debate in 1913 centered on the financial crisis problem that had characterized the late nineteenth and early twentieth centuries. The public finance issue was a peripheral one in public discourse.

Modern economists have tended to view the rationale behind the Fed's creation in either–or terms. Either the Fed was created for seigniorage purposes or else it was created for financial crisis purposes. The modern consensus, like the contemporary view, is that the fundamental purpose was to alleviate financial crises.

This chapter has rejected the either–or dichotomy. Simply put, a change in public financing requirements allowed the monetary environment to be restructured in a way that addressed the financial crisis problem. The founders created a competitive reserve bank system and replaced the government bond collateral requirement behind notes with a commercial paper collateral requirement. Interestingly, the impetus was a *reduction* in seigniorage requirements. The traditional seigniorage rationale has been turned on its head. The congressional intent in 1913 was to create a Federal Reserve System as an engine of monetary restraint, not as an engine of inflation.

External conditions changed rapidly in the last half of 1914 and the first half of 1915. By the middle of 1915, it was clear that the United States would participate in the war effort although the extent of its participation was uncertain. Given what amounted to a permanent increase in government spending, tax rates and seigniorage rates should increase. The difficulty the

Fed faced at this time was that the straitjacket imposed at its birth precluded the production of significant amounts of seigniorage.

The wartime emergency, however, made it possible to escape the straitjacket. The policy adjustment was twofold. One margin of adjustment was the gold reserve ratio. On an informal basis, Federal Reserve banks pursued less vigorously a policy which had resulted in a one-for-one backing of their monetary liabilities with gold.[7] By the end of 1916 the gold reserve ratio had fallen from opening day levels of 100 percent to around 70 percent. Then, in June 1917 the United States officially entered the war. With the degree of participation no longer a matter of conjecture, the Federal Reserve Act was amended in a way that would officially sanction a less than 100 percent gold reserve ratio. As described by Fishe, "the note issue power of the Federal Reserve in July 1917 was estimated to have increased by $1,875 million because of these amendments" (Fishe, 1991, p. 313).[8]

The new gold policy gave rise to a second margin of adjustment: a preferential discount rate policy. Under legislation also passed in 1917, the Board was to offer a preferential rate on loans backed by government bonds. The preferential rate was substantially below market rates and led to a run up in discount loans. Loans by reserve banks rose from $20 million in early 1917 to about $2 billion at the end of the policy in September 1921. My interpretation of the preferential policy is that it represented the means by which Fed management made payments (the "T" in chapter 2) to the Treasury for the right to run the Fed. The policy allowed the Treasury to capture the excess Fed revenue made possible by the reduction in the gold reserve.

The period following World War I was a special one in Federal Reserve history. Reserve banks found themselves in a position where their policies were not shackled by pre-existing constraints. In particular, they faced neither the prewar constraint of a 100 percent specie ratio, nor the wartime constraint of a preferential rate policy. The interesting issue was how the reserve banks would operate in the new monetary environment. The conventional view is that for most of the 1920s reserve bank decision makers exercised their new found freedom in a way that tended to stabilize the economy. The emphasis is on the fortuitous circumstances that placed individuals with strong leadership skills in positions of authority.

The theme developed in the next three chapters challenges the conventional view. The personality of Fed decision makers does not play an important role in this account; that is, Fed policy is not governed by happenstance. Instead, the story is one of how market forces come into play. According to the microeconomics approach Fed policy in the 1920s is as predictable as Fed policy during the straitjacket era. The tight constraints imposed by a 100 percent gold reserve and a wartime financing policy are replaced by the tight constraints imposed by competition.

Chapters 4 and 5 apply the market approach to the 1920s to shed light on two controversial Fed policy issues: (1) the role of seasonal movements in reserves in alleviating financial panics and (2) the implications of competitive open market operations for the over issue of money. In chapter 4, it becomes useful to introduce the details of the correspondent banking system as a way of illustrating how reserve bank interest payments were passed down through the different levels of the private banking system in the 1920s. In chapter 5, the emphasis is on how independently conducted open market operations in the early 1920s served to reduce the cost to private banks of holding reserves. While some preliminary tests are conducted in these chapters, more comprehensive tests are postponed to chapter 6 where the implications of the micro model are tested against the conclusions of more conventional accounts.

4 Interest on reserves and reserve smoothing in a correspondent banking system

4.1. Introduction

Economists have recently renewed their interest in the effects of the founding of the Federal Reserve on the frequency of financial panics. Much of this interest stems from work by Miron (1986) which attributes financial panics before 1914 to strains on the banking system caused by seasonal spikes in market interest rates. Miron argues that the founders created a system that directed Federal Reserve officials to use their discretion to supply reserves to the banking system during periods of seasonal strain. A properly timed discretionary policy reduces seasonal movements in interest rates and reduces the probability of bank failures. Miron's work has given rise to what I refer to as the new consensus, or new traditional, view of the founding of the Fed.[1]

This chapter emphasizes that the new consensus view differs fundamentally from the original conception of the Fed. For one thing, the founders tended to take seriously the gold standard constraints within which the newly created Fed would operate (Timberlake, 1978, pp. 221–2). These constraints would limit the ability of the Fed to control the interest rate. The founders' challenge, therefore, was to formulate a solution to the financial crisis problem that did not rely on interest rate control.

The key to their solution, I argue, was section 16 of the Federal Reserve Act which created the Fed as a national clearinghouse and granted it a right not possessed by private clearinghouses – the right to create reserves in the form of currency. As pointed out in the previous chapter, however, currency issue was restricted in the early years of the System. It was not until after World War I, when the straitjacket on reserve banks was relaxed, that reserve banks were able to take advantage of section 16 and provide an elastic currency.

The critical preconditions for an elastic currency supply are that reserve banks be subject to a less than 100 percent specie requirement and that the government's financing requirements not be too large. Under these circumstances the exemption from the restriction on currency issue would offer the Fed the opportunity to earn revenue which could be directly passed along to the large member banks and indirectly to the non-member banks via the correspondent system. One way to rebate the earnings to members would be through an in-kind payment of check-clearing services. Another way would be through below market discount loans. For instance, a discount subsidy could be provided to member banks simply by keeping the discount rate constant during autumn when market interest rates typically rose. The discount subsidy would reduce the strain on the banking system so that the probability of a financial panic would not rise significantly. Accordingly, the financial crisis problem would be resolved in an automatic, non-discretionary way.

The next section provides a historical overview of the currency elasticity issue in a gold standard setting with a correspondent banking system and relates it to the financial crisis problem. Section 4.3 extends the basic model of chapter 2 to the correspondent banking system and section 4.4 contrasts the role of private and public clearinghouses. Section 4.5 traces the evolution of the Federal Reserve System over its early years and shows that by the end of World War I the necessary preconditions for an elastic currency supply were in place. Section 4.6 offers concluding comments. The objective throughout this chapter is to model the financial crisis problem and its solution in a way that is faithful to the founders' view that the correspondent banking system, gold standard constraints, and the currency issue rights of the reserve banks were to be important elements in the Federal Reserve System.

4.2 Historical overview of an elastic money

Before the founding of the Federal Reserve, the correspondent banking system was generally perceived as playing an important role in the propagation of a financial crisis. The National Banking Act of 1864 classified national banks into three categories: redemption city banks in New York City, redemption city banks outside New York City, and non-redemption banks (country banks). The Act required New York City banks to hold a 25 percent reserve in lawful money (specie or greenbacks) against their note and deposit liabilities. The redemption city banks outside New York City also faced a 25 percent requirement, but they could hold half of the required amount as balances at New York City banks. Country banks were required to hold a 15 percent reserve, three-fifths of which could be held as balances at redemption banks. In terms of a vault cash requirement, therefore, New York City banks faced the full 25 percent requirement, redemption city banks outside New York City faced a 12.5 percent requirement, and country banks faced a requirement of only 6 percent. Finally, state agencies set reserve requirements for banks choosing state over national charters. These requirements were generally less stringent than the national ones with many states imposing no requirements or allowing state banks to count bankers' balances as reserves.[2]

City banks in the large financial centers tended to form private clearing-houses. As defined by W.E. Spahr, "a clearing house is an association of banks, ordinarily voluntary, to simplify and facilitate settlements of balances among the banks, and to serve as a medium for united action upon all questions affecting their common welfare" (1926, p. 70). The most well-known association was the New York Clearing House. For the settlement of transactions, the New York City banks held deposits at the Clearing House and/or scrip issued by the Clearing House. A bank that had a net "due to" position with respect to other members at settlement time could exchange its balances or scrip at the Clearing House for specie or currency (or more directly use its own holdings of specie and currency) and then send the specie or currency to the Clearing House for distribution among members. A major purpose of the New York Clearing House, and other regional clearinghouses, was to provide a liquidity guarantee. The Clearing House guaranteed that its deposit and scrip liabilities would be redeemable into the dominant money of the economy, either specie or a suitable currency substitute, and that members with claims on net "due to" banks at settlement time would immediately receive that amount in the form of the dominant money. If a member bank's net "due to" position exceeded its reserves (deposits at the Clearing House, scrip, currency, and specie), then the Clearing House would guarantee delivery of funds by discounting the "due to" bank's high quality paper.[3]

The reserves of the New York City banks consisted primarily of vault cash which did not pay interest. In contrast, other banks held a large portion of their reserves in forms that did pay interest. For instance, banks holding deposits (bankers' balances) at New York City banks typically received a fixed rate of 2 percent. While the New York City banks could supplement this explicit rate by providing correspondent services like check-clearing at below cost or loans at below market rates, the general view was that the overall return to banks outside New York City from holding bankers' balances did not vary substantially in the short run.

The correspondent system resulted in a concentration of reserves in the financial centers and seasonal movements of reserves into and out of the centers.[4] As explained by O.M.W. Sprague, market rates on loans in the local markets of country banks would be relatively low during periods of inactive business (winter and summer) and "temporarily idle funds would be attracted to the money centers by the interest to be secured for bankers' deposits" (1913, p. 128). The New York banks tended to invest these funds in the relatively illiquid call loan market as a way of earning a relatively high rate of return. During periods of active trade (spring and autumn) market rates tended to rise and country banks would withdraw funds from bankers' deposits held in New York banks. While the seasonal movement in bankers' balances would pose no special problems during "normal" years, it did place country banks and the entire banking system in a more fragile position during the autumn active-trading season (Sprague, 1910, p. 127). At this time bankers' balances, which were the primary source of funds for city banks and the primary reserves of country banks, would be relatively low. If some economy-wide shock resulted in unanticipated withdrawals from country banks, then country banks would experience a shortage of reserves. Moreover, as country banks cashed-in their bankers' balances, the city banks, whose assets were tied up in the call loan market, would find it costly to cover the unexpected withdrawals on such short notice. Because both country and city banks would be in highly illiquid positions, the probability of financial panic was relatively high during the active season.

A number of commentators pointed to the interest payment on bankers' balances as the source of the problem. They reasoned that, if city banks did not pay interest, then reserves would not be attracted to the center in the first place. Instead of holding bankers' balances, country banks would be more inclined to hold vault cash as reserves. A prohibition of interest payment on bankers' balances, therefore, would serve to shift the composition of reserves toward the highly liquid vault cash component. Furthermore, once relieved from the interest cost on bankers' balances, city banks would not be as anxious to seek out investments in the risky call loan market (Sprague, 1910, pp. 91–7; West, 1977, chapter 2).

At a more fundamental level, the financial crisis problem was attributed to an inelastic currency – in particular, the absence of any mechanism within the correspondent system which would serve to augment the nominal supply of currency during periods of seasonal stringency (see Sprague, 1913, chapter 3; for other pre-Fed sources see Friedman and Schwartz, 1963, pp. 168–72, 189–96). Currency tended to be inelastic across seasons because of several legal restrictions on currency issue by the banking system. For one thing, federal legislation passed in 1865 required that national bank notes be backed by US government securities and imposed a 10 percent tax on notes issued by banks other than national banks (for example, state banks). Perhaps more important, the National Banking Act of 1864 did not sanction clearinghouse currency and any attempt by clearinghouses to issue circulating currency legally should have been covered by the 10 percent tax imposed in 1865. Except for emergencies, when authorities tended to ignore the law, clearinghouses did not issue such currency (Spahr, 1926, p. 161; White, 1983, p. 77).

The early commentators who attributed the financial crisis problem to the restrictions on currency issue offered several remedies. The most radical approach called for placing a central clearinghouse at the top of the banking system with an exemption from the legal restrictions. According to one variant of this approach, the central clearinghouse's main task would be to formalize the 1902–6 policy of Treasury Secretary Leslie Shaw, who attempted to use excess reserves of the Treasury to smooth interest rates (Timberlake, 1978, pp. 175–9). According to another view, however, the gold standard would impose tight constraints on the ability of a central authority to control market interest rates.[5] Still, an ordinary clearinghouse might be able to reduce the probability of financial crisis if given the opportunity to undertake its clearinghouse functions to the fullest extent possible. A clearinghouse, whose currency issue was not legally restricted, may have both the capability and the incentive to use its tools – most notably discount loans to city banks – to reduce the seasonal strain on the banking system.

The historical overview has discussed the source of the financial crisis problem from the perspective of those who were instrumental in the founding of the Fed. One version of this "old" tradition focused on the legal restrictions placed on financial institutions in the correspondent system as the primary source of the financial crisis problem. Under this interpretation, the payment of interest on bankers' balances was not the culprit, but instead it was federal law which restricted the issue of currency by private banks and most important by private clearinghouses. Within this legal restriction camp, however, there was no widely agreed-upon policy prescription. In particular, there was no definitive analysis about how a public clearinghouse might be able to smooth the reserves of the banking system in a gold standard setting where the clearinghouse was unable to influence the market rate on loans.

Recent models of the financial crisis problem have downplayed the gold standard setting as well as a second factor that was central to the earlier analysis – the role of the correspondent system. Miron's oft-cited model is a prototype for this modern view. He models the interest rate as determined in the domestic loan market and treats a bank as an entity whose decisions are independent of decisions of the other financial institutions higher up in the hierarchy. According to this "new" tradition, the central bank wards off financial crises by smoothing market interest rates.

4.3 Modeling reserve smoothing in a correspondent banking system

My objective in this section is to model reserve smoothing in a way that brings to center stage the founders' emphasis on the correspondent system, gold standard constraints, and the role of legal restrictions on clearinghouses. The major insight, which was implicit in the founders' view but not rigorously formulated, is that the elimination of legal restrictions on the Fed would reduce Fed costs and induce the Fed to pass these savings along to the large city banks, who were its primary members, in such a way as to smooth their reserve holding costs. Also, in a correspondent setting, market pressures would cause the city banks to pass the savings further down the banking hierarchy to the country banks. The end result is that a non-legally restricted Fed would directly smooth city bank holding cost and indirectly smooth country bank holding cost without affecting market interest rates.

The basic set-up is a refinement of the model presented in chapter 2. In that model there were two types of financial institutions: banks and clearinghouses. Here we add a third type by separating private banks into country and city banks. The model simplifies the reserve holding decisions of the three institutions. The country banks hold reserves at the city banks in the form of bankers' balances. The city banks hold reserves in the form of deposits at the clearinghouse or possibly specie in their vaults. The clearinghouse holds specie as reserves.

For the country bank, I use a variation of the profit function from chapter 2 (see equation 2.2). In particular

$$\Pi_B = iS_B + bBB - (w_B^2/2)[(BB/D) - 1]^2, \tag{4.1}$$

where Π_B is expected profit, i is the interest rate on bank assets, S_B is the planned quantity of bank assets, b is the interest rate on bankers' balances at a city bank, BB is planned bankers' balances, w_B^2 is the variance of withdrawals from the country bank, and D is expected deposits. Country bank costs are given by $(w_B^2/2)[(BB/D) - 1]^2$, with bankers' balances serving as reserves. A major difference between (4.1) and (2.2) is that the country bank does not obtain loans from a reserve bank.

The country bank maximizes expected profit subject to the constraint, $BB + S_B = D$. The bank's optimal amount of reserves is

$$BB^* = D[1 - (c_B D/w_B^2)], \tag{4.2}$$

where c_B is the country bank's opportunity cost of holding a dollar at the city bank. Because country banks do not borrow from a reserve bank, c_B equals $i - b$.[6]

A Miron-like interpretation of the pre-1914 financial crisis problem can be illustrated with equation (4.2). First note that Miron did not consider the possibility of an interest payment on reserves; that is, $b = 0$. Also, Miron assumed that the interest rate on bank assets ("loans") was determined in the banking system by the aggregate supply and demand for bank assets such that i tended to rise in the autumn. Given that $b = 0$, then $c_B = i$ and the direct effect of the increase in the interest rate on loans was to raise the cost of holding reserves. Because the country bank would respond by reducing its reserve-deposit ratio, it would be more exposed to unexpected deposit withdrawals and so the frequency of panics would be relatively high during the autumn.

In contrast to Miron, I adhere to the view, prominent among many at the time of the Fed's creation, that the gold standard would remain intact and that the interest rate on loans would be determined in a world market. I also contend that ignoring the interconnections between country banks and other financial institutions in the correspondent system is an important omission. Extending the model to city banks and ultimately to clearing-houses shows that country banks generally receive interest on balances at city banks and that the seasonal behavior of b depends on whether clearing-houses are legally restricted from issuing their own currency.

The prototype city bank is one located in a financial center, like New York City. Using the equation (4.1) formulation for the country bank as a general guide, the expected profit function of the New York City bank (N) can be given by

$$\Pi_N = iS_N + r_N R_N - (w_N^2/2)[(R_N/BB) - 1]^2 - bBB - dL_C, \qquad (4.3)$$

where L_N is loans of the city bank, R_N is city bank reserves, r_N is the interest rate received on reserves, w_N^2 is the variance of withdrawals by country banks of their bankers' balances, L_C is loans from the clearinghouse to the city bank, and d is the interest rate on these loans.[7] A distinctive feature of (4.3) is that there are two sources of funds for the city bank – deposits of country banks and loans from the clearinghouse. Even if the clearinghouse paid no interest on reserves ($r_N = 0$), it could subsidize city banks by providing them with below market discount loans ($d < i$).

The city bank is subject to the constraint that $L_N + R_N = BB + L_C$, where, as was discussed in chapter 2, the amount of loans extended by the clearing-house is determined by the amount of specie it must hold to provide the liquidity guarantee. Again, letting ρ represent the proportion of specie to clearinghouse liabilities, clearinghouse loans can be given by $L_C = R_N(1-\rho)$ and the city bank constraint simplifies to $L_N = BB - \rho R_N$.[8] Making these substitutions into (4.3) and rearranging gives the city bank profit maximization problem

$$\text{Max } \Pi_N = (i-b)BB - [i\rho - r + d(1-\rho)]R - (w_N^2/2)[(R/BB) - 1]^2, \quad (4.4)$$

where the subscripts have been omitted when the intention is clear.

The city bank has two choice variables, the interest rate on bankers' balances, b, and the amount of reserves, R, to hold at the clearinghouse. In choosing the interest rate on bankers' balances, the city bank must consider the country bank's response. Equation (4.2) shows that the country bank increases bankers' balances at the city bank with increases in the interest rate on these balances. Substituting BB^* from equation (4.2) for BB in equation (4.4), the city bank's optimization problem results in the general solutions

$$R^* = BB^*[1 - (c_N BB^*/w_N^2)], \tag{4.5}$$

$$b^* = i - \{[(w_B^2/D) + c_N - (c_N^2 D/w_N^2)]/[2 - (c_N^2 D^2/w_B^2 w_N^2)]\}, \tag{4.6}$$

where $c_N = [i\rho - r + d(1-\rho)]$. Equation (4.5) is analogous to the country bank's reserve equation with c_N representing the city bank's opportunity cost of holding reserves at the clearinghouse.

Equation (4.6) challenges Miron's assumption that the interest rate on a country bank's reserves is zero, and provides the first fundamental insight of the correspondent model.

Proposition 1: The interest rate a city bank pays on bankers' balances generally will be some non-zero amount that depends on the exogenous parameters, i, w_B^2, w_N^2, ρ, and D, as well as on the rates, r and d, set by the clearinghouse.

Because seasonal movements in b are influenced by the possible seasonality of r and d, the behavior of clearinghouses becomes a key element in understanding the financial crisis problem.

4.4 The role of a clearinghouse

Consider a generic clearinghouse that, while not necessarily having any real-world counterpart, serves as a reference for assessing two special cases: a legally restricted private clearinghouse and a non-legally restricted national clearinghouse. The generic clearinghouse is of the type considered in chapter 2. It clears checks for its members, offers discount loans to members, and provides a liquidity guarantee that each member's deposits at the clearinghouse will be redeemed instantly in the dominant money.

The costs of a clearinghouse stem from the check-clearing services it provides and from any explicit interest payments it makes on city bank reserves and the revenues stem from its discount loans and any check-clearing fees it charges. Clearinghouse profits can be given by $\Pi = dL_C - rR$, and the balance sheet constraint by $L_C + P_G G = R$ where P_G is the cost of specie in terms of units of output and G is units of specie. For convenience, set $P_G = 1$, so that $G = \rho R$. Making the appropriate substitutions gives the clearinghouse's maximization problem as

$$\text{Max } \Pi = BB^*[1 - (c_N BB^*/w_N^2)][d(1-\rho) - r]. \tag{4.7}$$

To further simplify the problem, assume that the clearinghouse is subject to a zero profit constraint. This constraint would arise if the clearinghouse operated in a contestable market. Alternatively, the zero profit constraint may be justified by the cooperative nature of the enterprise; the organizers of the clearinghouse, city banks, may desire that any excess revenue be transferred to them in the form of relatively high interest payments on reserves or relatively low discount rates on loans.

Under these circumstances, the clearinghouse must set r and d in (4.7) to satisfy the condition, $d(1-\rho)-r=0$. Making this substitution in equation (4.6) gives

$$i-(b^*)_{GC}=i\{(w_B^2/iD)+\rho[1-(\rho iD/w_N^2)]\}/\{2-[(\rho iD)^2/w_B^2 w_N^2]\}, \quad (4.8)$$

where the GC subscript indicates the solution with a generic clearinghouse. Stipulating that bank reserve ratios be between 0 and 1 insures that the {} terms in equation (4.8) are positive and therefore that the rate on bankers' balances is less than the loan rate. An important factor that determines the particular bankers' balance rate set by the city bank is the ability of its clearinghouse to substitute between currency and specie, as reflected in the reserve ratio, ρ.

In keeping with the correspondent banking system as it existed before 1914, assume that a private clearinghouse faces a legal restriction in providing the liquidity guarantee. At one extreme, the legal code may preclude the clearinghouse from issuing its own currency under any conceivable set of events. More generally, the legal code may simply impose conditions on the issue of currency. For instance, the legal code may place a ceiling on the amount of clearinghouse currency or it may authorize currency issues only during emergencies.

At this point, assume that the law prohibits the private clearinghouse from issuing currency under any circumstances. Given the liquidity guarantee, the private clearinghouse would have no choice but to back city bank deposits one-for-one with specie implying a balance sheet constraint of $G=R$ and $L_C=0$. This leads to

Proposition 2: For a legally restricted competitive clearinghouse (LC), $\rho=1$, which according to the zero profit condition, $d(1-\rho)-r=0$, requires that $(r)_{LC}=0$; that is, $(r^e)_{LC}=0$ and $(f)_{LC}=k$. As a result, there is no interest rate advantage to the city bank from holding reserves as deposits at the clearinghouse versus specie. The city bank's reserve cost, $(c_N)_{LC}=i-(r)_{LC}=i$, moves one-for-one with seasonal movements in i.

Because of the legal restriction, city bank deposits generate no earnings for the clearinghouse. The clearinghouse is unable to pay interest on these deposits, either explicitly through r^e or implicitly through a subsidized check-clearing fee. With no interest rate advantage to holding deposits at the clearinghouse, city banks typically will hold specie and the city bank's opportunity cost of holding reserves will move seasonally.

The clearinghouse's rate-setting strategy will feed through the correspondent system and affect the interest rate that a city bank pays on bankers' balances. Substituting $\rho = 1$ in equation (4.8) results in

$$i - (b^*)_{LC} = i[(w_B^2/iD) + 1 - (iD/w_N^2)]/[2 - (i^2D^2/w_B^2w_N^2)]. \qquad (4.9)$$

The country bank's opportunity cost of holding reserves can be given by the general function $(c_B)_{LC} = i - (b^*)_{LC} = f(i, w_B^2, w_N^2, D)$. Generally, an increase in i produces a less than one-for-one increase in $(b^*)_{LC}$, implying that $(c_B)_{LC}$ rises with i.[9]

Equation (4.9), in conjunction with equations (4.2) and (4.5), provides the basis for a third insight of the correspondent model.

Proposition 3: With a legally restricted competitive clearinghouse, the country bank's reserve cost, $(c_B)_{LC}$, and the reserve aggregates, $(R^*)_{LC}$ and $(BB^*)_{LC}$, respond to seasonal movements in i.

Compare propositions 2 and 3 with Miron's pre-1914 setup. Miron did not distinguish between different types of banks and simply *assumed* an inflexible (zero) interest rate on reserves. In contrast, I have derived a zero interest rate on the reserves of city banks and a somewhat inflexible interest rate on the reserves of country banks as *implications* of maximizing behavior in a correspondent setting which explicitly models the connections between the country banks, city banks, and legally restricted clearinghouses.

The limitations of Miron's model come to the forefront once the correspondent model is modified to allow for the possibility that the clearinghouse at the top does not face legal restrictions. Consider a national clearinghouse, call it the Fed, which is identical to the private clearinghouse except that it has the legal right to create reserves by creating currency. The right to issue currency allows the Fed to guarantee redemption of member bank (city bank) deposits into currency and to cover member bank short-falls of reserves even though it invests deposit funds in income-earning assets. These earnings provide a source for subsidizing member banks either through below market discount loans or more directly through an interest payment on bank deposits at the clearinghouse. Potentially, these subsidies could feed through the correspondent system and produce stronger seasonal movements in the interest rate on country bank reserves.

To explore this issue in the simplest way, and to make the contrast between a legally restricted private clearinghouse and the Fed as sharp as possible, assume that the Fed has an unattenuated right to create currency, that currency is a perfect substitute for specie as the dominant money, and that the cost of printing new currency is zero. Under these circumstances, the clearinghouse's liquidity guarantee to member banks requires no specie reserve; that is, $\rho=0$ and the balance sheet constraint (maintaining the assumption of no outstanding currency) simplifies to $L_C=R$.

We shall also continue to assume that the Fed, as a clearinghouse, is subject to a zero profit condition. This assumption may seem inappropriate with respect to a national clearinghouse since contestability is problematic in a nationalized setting. Nevertheless, the zero profit condition can be defended on a number of grounds. Most important, the founders of the Fed included provisions in the Federal Reserve Act which subjected the market for Fed money to considerable competitive pressures. Foremost among these were the provisions, outlined in chapter 3, granting each of the twelve reserve banks their own money production powers. If the Fed (the Fed Board) set a discount rate that provided reserve banks with supernormal profits, then each of the reserve banks would attempt to capture a larger market share by taking actions (for instance, by conducting open market operations) which would have the effect of lowering profit margins. The mere threat of independent adjustment would serve as an important constraint on systemwide profits.

The zero profit condition can also be defended as a simplifying assumption that does not affect the main results of the analysis. As long as reserve banks face some competitive pressures, even though they may not be operating in a perfectly contestable market, then the qualitative nature of the results derived in this section will continue to hold; that is, reserve banks will tend to pay interest on reserves and the cost to banks of holding reserves will tend to be smoother than otherwise. The critical point in this model is that reserve banks are not pure regional monopolists who refuse to make interest payments on reserves.

The simple zero profit assumption turns the Fed into a price-taker. The Fed must use the discount window to supply city banks with the amount of reserves they want at a discount rate and a rate of interest on reserves that leaves it with zero profits. To formally illustrate the price-taker results, set $\rho=0$ in the zero profit condition, $d(1-\rho)-r=0$. This results in $d=r$. The revenue generated by a discount loan is returned to the member banks in the form of an interest payment on reserves.[10] The only discretion the Fed has is at what level to set the discount rate and, given this rate, whether to pay interest on reserves explicitly at the rate r^e, implicitly at the rate $k-f$, or through a combination of explicit and implicit payments, such that $d=r=r^e+(k-f)$. In the simplified setting considered here, the full rate of return on reserves equals i, the sum of the discount rate subsidy, $i-d$, and the interest rate on reserves, r.[11]

Fed policy can be summarized by two propositions.

Proposition 4a: Unlike a legally restricted clearinghouse, the Fed (F) will tend to make below market rate discount loans, $0 < (d)_F < i$, and positive interest payments on reserves, $(r^e)_F > 0$ and/or $(f)_F < k$. The city bank's reserve cost, $(c_N)_F = (d)_F - (r)_F = 0$, does not move with seasonal movements in i.

Proposition 4b: If $(f)_F = (r^e)_F = 0$, then $(c_N)_F = (d)_F - k$ and the zero profit condition requires $(d)_F = k$.

Proposition 4a is a statement about general rate-setting strategy which says that the national clearinghouse must choose a d, r^e, and f combination that makes the city bank's reserve holding cost, $(d)_F - (r)_F$, zero. The general model determines only the difference $(d)_F - (r)_F$ and does not lead to determinate solutions for $(d)_F$, $(r^e)_F$, and $(f)_F$ separately. Proposition 4b is a special case that leads to a determinate discount rate. If the national clearinghouse charges no fee and pays no explicit interest on reserves, then, in order to make the reserve cost zero, the clearinghouse must set the discount rate equal to k, the per unit cost of member bank reserves. Treating k as a constant, the model implies that the discount rate does not move seasonally.

In order to determine how the Fed's exemption from the legal restriction feeds through the rest of the banking system, set $\rho = 0$ in equation (4.8) to get

$$i - (b^*)_F = w_B^2/2D. \tag{4.10}$$

The opportunity cost to country banks of holding reserves is independent of the loan rate. A comparison of equation (4.8) with (4.10) is the basis of

Proposition 5: Exempting a clearinghouse from the restriction on currency issue increases b; that is, $(b^*)_F \geq (b^*)_{LC}$. The exemption also causes $(b^*)_F$ to move one-for-one with i. Country bank reserve costs, $(c_B)_F$, and city and country bank reserves, $(R^*)_F$ and $(BB^*)_F$, do not respond to seasonal movements in i.

The result that $(b^*)_F \geq (b^*)_{LC}$ follows from the observation that when $w_N^2 = 0$, a city bank in a legally restricted setting is in the same position as the city bank in the Fed setting in that neither bank faces any costs associated with unexpected withdrawals. In this special case, $(b^*)_F = (b^*)_{LC}$. As w_N^2 rises, the legally restricted city bank's costs rise and it passes these costs along in the form of a lower interest payment.

Propositions 4a, 4b, and 5 summarize the key smoothing implications of the legal restriction model. Creation of a national clearinghouse in the form of the Fed smooths city and country bank reserve costs and smooths city and country bank reserves. As highlighted by 4b, a critical variable in this process may be the discount rate. Under certain circumstances, the Fed implements the smoothing policy simply by keeping the discount rate constant during seasons of increasing market loan rates. This helps alleviate the financial crisis problem even though the Fed may be unable to influence the market interest rate on loans in this model.[12]

4.5 Fed policy and the elasticity issue

The Fed's role in smoothing reserves, as summarized in propositions 1–5, centers on its currency issue rights relative to those of its private counterpart. Section 16 of the Federal Reserve Act is the key. It granted reserve banks the statutory authority to create their own monetary liabilities in the form of Federal Reserve notes and member bank deposits. This authority was not unrestricted, however. Section 11 of the Act stipulated a 40 percent gold reserve requirement against the Fed's monetary liabilities and when the reserve banks opened for business they operated on the basis of a 100 percent gold reserve (see chapter 3). Still, the Federal Reserve Act held out the promise of a reduction in the gold reserve at some future date which should work in the direction suggested by propositions 1–5. Most important, the overall level of subsidies to the banking system should increase even when there is no mechanism through which Fed policy affects the market interest rate on loans.[13]

This section provides a hierarchy of tests of the results contained in propositions 1–5. Start with propositions 2 and 4a which compare the general rate-setting policy of private clearinghouses before 1914 with the Fed's policy. Although private clearinghouses before 1914 differed in their rate-setting policies, general tendencies can be identified. Consistent with proposition 2, most of a member's reserves were held as vault cash (for example, specie) rather than deposits at the clearinghouse (Spahr, 1926, p. 135) and there is little indication that clearinghouses routinely extended below market discount loans to their members.[14] Most important, there is little indication that they offered a price break on check-clearing services; Gorton and Mullineaux (1987) note that clearinghouses typically required their members to share the full costs of check-clearing.

In contrast, member bank subsidies were a built-in feature of the Federal Reserve System. With respect to discount policy, sections 13 and 14d of the Federal Reserve Act created a real bills mechanism that allowed reserve banks to discount "notes, drafts, and bills of exchange arising out of actual commercial transactions" (section 13) at discount rates to be established "with a view of accommodating commerce and business" (section 14d). The Act assigned the locus of decision-making power to the individual reserve banks with general oversight by the Federal Reserve Board. After the straitjacket phase, the reserve banks liberally extended discount loans to member banks, making discount loans a primary source of reserve bank earnings (see Board of Governors, 1943, table 100, p. 368). While the discount rate

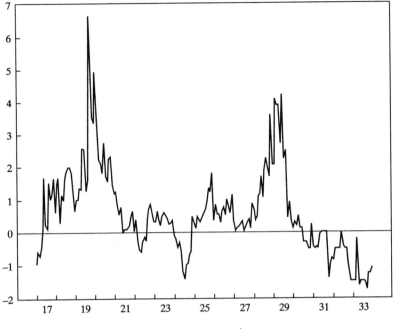

Figure 4.1 Call and discount rate spread

was initially above the call rate of interest, figure 4.1 shows that from 1917 until the Great Depression the discount rate was often somewhat below the call rate; even in those years (1917, 1921, 1922, 1924) when the discount rate was above the call rate for a number of months, it was below the call rate by the end of the year. Consistent with proposition 4a, discount loans were at least a modest source of subsidies to the banking system.

Proposition 4a also predicts explicit or implicit interest payments on reserves. The Federal Reserve Act did not authorize explicit payments but did officially sanction an in-kind payment by allowing the Reserve Board to set the fee that reserve banks could charge for services to member banks at a level below costs. At first, the problem of earnings (see chapter 3) forced reserve banks to set check-clearing fees to cover costs. Therefore, in-kind interest payments were not important at the birth of the Fed. In 1918, however, the Fed reduced check-clearing fees to zero (Spahr, 1926, pp. 192–3; Duprey and Nelson, 1986, p. 27) so that starting in 1918 member banks received interest payments in the form of "free" check-clearing services.

The crucial issue is not whether the reserve banks offered discount subsidies and in-kind payments on reserves, but whether the magnitude of these payments were economically meaningful. Were they of such magnitude to have significantly enhanced the stability of the banking system?

Consider first the in-kind component of the full rate of return. The size of the in-kind component would be conditioned by the amount of Fed revenue the reserve banks spent on member bank services versus the amount transferred to the government. Table 4.1 provides a complete account of Fed transfers over the period from 1917 to 1979. The interwar period stands out as one where little revenue was transferred. Most of the revenue was used to cover Fed operating expenses.

Another factor influencing the size of the in-kind component is the extent to which Fed operating expenses were targeted to member banks. Throughout its existence, the major Fed expense categories have been check-clearing and currency services provided to member banks. Still, the question arises as to how much of these outlays represent value to member banks and how much monopoly rents to the Fed banks.

Estimating the in-kind component proves less troublesome over the period 1922–28 as compared with earlier or later periods. For one thing, the end-points, 1922 and 1928, correspond to the termination of the preferential discount rate policy and to the beginning of the depression. Second, figure 4.1 shows that, even though monthly discount rates were sometimes above and sometimes below monthly commercial paper rates, on an average annual basis the two roughly equaled each other. Third, the period is generally considered to be a relatively competitive one so that monopoly rents would tend to be low.

Based on these observations, assume that the average annual discount rate equaled the market rate and that reserve banks faced a zero profit constraint. Then the payment of interest by reserve banks from 1922–8 can be characterized as follows. When a city bank deposited a dollar of reserves, the Fed set aside ρ in gold and invested the remainder in earning assets. The earning assets generated revenue, a part of which may have been transferred to the Treasury. Competition would assure that the amount not transferred would be paid out to the member banks in the form of in-kind payments.

Table 4.2 provides an estimate of this "competitive" in-kind rate of return on an annual average basis. Column (1) gives the systemwide reserve ratio, column (2) gives the rate of return of Fed assets (current Fed income/ Fed earning assets), column (3) reports transfers to the Treasury as a proportion of Fed earning assets, column (4) gives the *net* rate of return of Fed assets (columns (2)–(3)), column (5) gives the interest rate on reserves (column (4) $\times$ (1−ρ), column (6) reports the commercial paper rate, and column (7) reports the spread between commercial paper rate and the interest rate on reserves (columns (6)−(5)).

Given that the discount rate approximated the market rate, the spread between the market rate and the reserve rate in table 4.2 represents the cost

Table 4.1 *Fed Treasury Transfers*

Year	Transfers ($billions)	Transfers as percent of government receipts*	Year	Transfers ($billions)	Transfers as percent of government receipts
1917	0.001				
18	—				
19	0.003				
1920	0.061		1950	0.197	0.394
21	0.060		51	0.255	0.397
22	0.011		52	0.292	0.434
23	0.004		53	0.343	0.490
24	0.0001		54	0.276	0.433
25	0.00006		55	0.252	0.347
26	0.0008		56	0.402	0.515
27	0.0002		57	0.543	0.663
28	0.003		58	0.524	0.666
29	0.004	0.105	59	0.911	1.014
1930	0.00002	0.0007	1960	0.897	0.933
31	—	—	61	0.687	0.701
32	0.002	0.117	62	0.799	0.752
33	—	—	63	0.880	0.769
34	—	—	64	1.582	1.377
35	0.0003	0.008	65	1.297	1.043
36	0.0002	0.004	66	1.649	1.163
37	0.0002	0.003	67	1.907	1.267
38	0.0001	0.002	68	2.464	1.413
39	0.00002	0.0003	69	3.019	1.534
1940	0.00008	0.0009	1970	3.494	1.821
41	0.0001	0.0006	71	3.357	1.691
42	0.0002	0.0009	72	3.231	1.420
43	0.0002	0.0005	73	4.341	1.678
44	0.0003	0.0007	74	5.550	1.928
45	0.0002	0.0005	75	5.382	1.873
46	0.00007	0.0002	76	5.870	1.769
47	0.075	0.174	77	5.937	1.582
48	0.167	0.386	78	7.006	1.623
49	0.193	0.499	79	9.279	1.880

Note:
*Receipt data not available on a calendar year basis before 1929.
Source: Goodfriend and Hargraves (1983).

Table 4.2 *Annual interest rates on reserves, 1922–1928*

Year	ρ (1)	Income/ Fed assets (2)	Transfers/ Fed assets (3)	Net asset rate (4)	Reserve rate (5)	Paper rate (6)	Spread (7)
1922	0.725	0.038	0.008	0.030	0 .008	0.045	0.037
1923	0.753	0.042	0.003	0.039	0.010	0.050	0.040
1924	0.730	0.031	0.000	0.031	0.008	0.040	0.032
1925	0.690	0.030	0.000	0.030	0.009	0.040	0.031
1926	0.714	0.036	0.000	0.036	0.010	0.043	0.033
1927	0.664	0.027	0.000	0.027	0.009	0.041	0.032
1928	0.663	0.036	0.001	0.035	0.013	0.049	0.036

Source: Board of Governors (1943).

to banks of holding reserves. For the period as a whole, the average interest rate on reserves was 1 percent (0.010) and the average commercial paper rate was 4.4 percent (0.044). Therefore, the reserve rate reduced the cost to member banks of holding reserves from 4.4 percent to 3.4 percent. Put differently, it reduced the holding cost by more than 20 percent. These estimates suggest that the in-kind payments that member banks received on reserves in the aftermath of World War I were not trivial.

The next empirical issue concerns the seasonal behavior of the reserve rate. Here, the reserve banks' discount policy is the focus of interest. Given that the preconditions ($f=r^e=0$) for proposition 4b hold, the major insight is that movements in the discount rate should be tied to movements in the Fed's costs (services provided) per unit of member bank reserves; that is, $d=k$.[15] In the long run there may be substantial variation in k and therefore substantial variation in d. As an empirical matter, however, I assume there is little short-run fluctuation in k. Under this circumstance, the testable implication of the correspondent model is that the Fed's discount rate is not seasonal. During the autumn, when the call rate of interest tends to rise, the discount rate stays constant and the rate of subsidy to the banking system automatically increases.

Figure 4.2 plots the seasonal pattern for the call rate of interest, the discount rate, and the spread between the call and discount rates from 1917–28.[16] The call rate exhibits a seasonal pattern, although the seasonality is less pronounced than before 1914. Because the discount rate is relatively constant throughout the year, the call/discount rate spread series roughly corresponds to the call rate series. Most notably, reserve banks do not increase the discount rate near the end-of-the-year when the call rate is rising. Table 4.3 formally shows that the call rate and the call/discount rate

Table 4.3 *Tests for seasonality in the call rate, the discount rate, the rate spread, and bankers' balances*[a]

Variable	Period	F	Q
Call rate	1917–28	2.25	9.07[b]
Discount rate	1917–28	0.86 (0.58)	1.76
Rate spread	1917–28	2.21 (0.02)	2.83[b]
Bankers' balances	1922–8	0.72 (0.71)	0.68

Notes:
[a]Significance level is in parentheses.
[b]Exceeds 0.05 critical value.
Source: Board of Governors (1943).

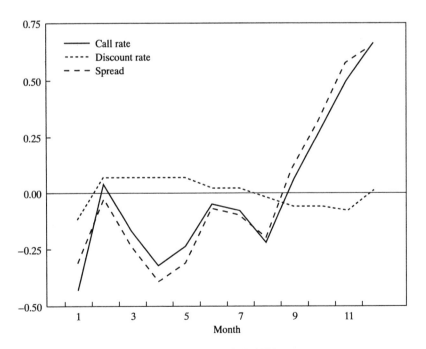

Figure 4.2 Seasonal interest rates, 1917–1928

spread patterns are statistically significant. Movements in the discount rate are not significant.

Statistical significance is one thing, but economic significance another. Consider the last quarter of a "typical" year. Figure 4.2 shows that subsidies tended to be 0.35 of a percentage point higher in October than in the rest of the year, 0.55 higher in November, and 0.65 higher in December. To place these monthly subsidies in context, note that the average annual holding cost for the 1922–8 period was 3.4 percent (average annual market rate of 4.4 percent less the average annual reserve rate of 1 percent). The seasonal subsidies, therefore, served to reduce the holding cost of reserves during October by about 10 percent (0.35/3.4), during November by about 15 percent (0.55/3.4), and during December by about 20 percent (0.65/3.4). On this basis, the subsidies appear to have been large enough to have reduced the seasonal strain on the banking system by a meaningful amount.

Another set of predictions, as summarized in propositions 1, 3, and 5, pertain to how the absence of private clearinghouse subsidies and the presence of Fed subsidies affect the rest of the banking system. The predictions of the correspondent model are that New York banks would pay interest on the reserves of country banks before and after 1914 (proposition 1); that the interest rate on reserves of country banks would tend to be higher after the Fed's creation (proposition 5); that the response of the interest rate on country bank reserves to seasonal movements in the market interest rate on loans would increase after the Fed's creation (propositions 3 and 5); and that the response of city and country bank reserves to seasonal movements in the market interest rate on loans would decrease after the Fed's creation (propositions 3 and 5).

Proposition 1 can easily be verified by noting that New York City banks typically paid an explicit interest rate of 2 percent on bankers' balances both before and after 1914. This piece of evidence, however, is not decisive in evaluating the prediction that on average b increased and became more seasonal after 1914. The problem here is that in the real world an explicit interest payment on reserves is one of many methods available to New York banks in transmitting clearinghouse subsidies to country banks. Other possibilities include below cost services and below cost loans provided by the New York banks to the country banks. While summary statistics are not readily available, informal evidence suggests that New York banks made more extensive use of these methods after the Fed's creation. In a study comparing the New York money market before and after 1914, James G. Smith (1932) concluded that "through the use of the Federal Reserve clearing system, the city banks have been able to improve and to diminish the cost of the services they offer correspondent banks in the way of clearances and the collection of items" (p. 281).

Table 4.4 *Tests of hypotheses of no change in seasonal movements of the call rate and reserve aggregates in 1922 (sample period, 1919–1928)*

Variable	F	Significance level
Call rate	3.67	0.0001
New York City reserves	0.81	0.64
New York City loan reserve	0.91	0.54

Source: Board of Governors, *Banking and Monetary Statistics* (1943).

Propositions 3 and 5 also imply that a seasonal change in the loan rate will affect reserve aggregates of city and country banks before 1914 but not after the Fed's creation. In contrast, Miron's model implies that a change in the loan rate will affect reserve aggregates in both periods. The difference stems from the definition of the opportunity cost of holding reserves: for Miron the cost is the loan rate and for the legal restriction model it is the loan rate less any subsidy rate.

Miron (1986) documented that *in general* loan rates were less seasonal after the Fed's creation and that this corresponded to less seasonality in loans, reserves, and the loan–reserve ratio. Likewise, Smith (1932) focused on bankers' balances and documented that balances in New York City banks were less seasonal after the Fed's creation. The important point is that these findings are consistent not only with Miron's model but also with the microeconomics model of correspondent banking since the cost of holding reserves is smoother in each model. The empirical challenge is to identify a period when the two cost measures behaved differently.

As will be discussed in chapter 6, Holland and Toma (1991) have identified such a period. They found that the call rate was not seasonal before 1922, but exhibited a significant seasonal pattern over the sub period 1922–8. With the call rate representing the cost to banks of holding reserves in Miron's model, seasonal movements in reserve aggregates should be more pronounced starting in 1922. In the micro model, seasonal movements in reserve aggregates should not differ significantly before and after 1922 since Fed interest payments to banks would be expected to vary with the call rate.

To provide some evidence on this issue, I tested whether the seasonality of two reserve aggregates – New York City banks' reserve balances at the Fed and New York City banks' loan–reserve ratio – changed in 1922 along with the change in the seasonality of the call rate of interest. The results are summarized in table 4.4. Seasonal fluctuations in these reserve aggregates did not increase in the sub-period 1922–8. Also, I tested the seasonality of bankers' balances at New York City banks for the critical sub-period and found that bankers' balances did not fluctuate seasonally. Overall, the results are consistent with the micro proposition that routine Fed interest payments during periods of seasonally high loan rates smoothed reserve-holding costs and reserve aggregates in the banking system.

4.6 Concluding remarks

This chapter has revived a prominent early conception of the Fed's founding by developing a model of the correspondent banking system which attributes the pre-1914 financial crisis problem to a legal restriction on the ability of private clearinghouses to issue their own currency as backing for the deposits of member banks. The Federal Reserve Act placed fewer restrictions on the currency issue rights of the reserve banks. The reserve banks, however, were not in a position to take advantage of these rights until the end of World War I. The correspondent model implies that at this time the reserve banks would pass along their cost saving to the rest of the banking system thereby smoothing reserve-holding costs and reducing the probability of financial crisis in a way that did not require manipulation of market interest rates. Evidence presented from the decade of the 1920s tends to support the major predictions of the correspondent model.

5 Competitive open market operations

5.1 Introduction

The elasticity of Fed money was not the only issue of interest in the decade following World War I. An issue of equal importance was whether reserve banks' use of their individual money production powers, now that they no longer faced a 100 percent gold reserve nor were shackled by a wartime financing policy, would result in an over issue of money. In addressing the over issue problem, Federal Reserve historians, such as Chandler (1958), Friedman and Schwartz (1963), and Wheelock (1991), have recognized the special attributes of the early 1920s environment. They have tended to view the period from 1921 to 1923 as one of profit-seeking reserve banks actively competing with each other. In the words of Friedman and Schwartz, "open market operations were not yet coordinated but were being carried out primarily to increase earnings rather than as general credit policy" (1963, pp. 281–2).

Conventional wisdom holds that competitive reserve banks would be prone to over issue money. Speaking with specific reference to the early 1920s, D'Arista pointed to the likelihood that reserve banks would tend to "create easy money" (D'Arista, 1994, p. 74). In a more general context, Rolnick, Smith, and Weber (1993, 1994) have given the tendency of over issue by competitive money producers the generic label of a "seigniorage incentive problem" (Rolnick, Smith, and Weber, 1993, 1994).

The conventional wisdom can be contrasted with the microeconomics perspective presented in chapter 2. That model emphasized the market constraints on over issue. Simply put, competition in the reserve bank industry would be associated with monetary restraint and the absence of a seigniorage incentive problem.

The major objective of this chapter is to use the 1921–3 competitive episode to shed light on the over issue controversy. Sections 5.2 and 5.3 outline the implications of the conventional view in some detail and contrast these implications with those that emerge from the micro model. Section 5.4

extends the basic discount model of chapter 2 to competitive open market operations and section 5.5 presents an empirical overview which suggests that over issue was not a problem during the competitive period.

5.2 Conventional view

Conventional wisdom holds that competition among money producers in a unified monetary system, such as the Federal Reserve System, results in a seigniorage incentive problem characterized by overproduction of money. Overproduction occurs because the public treats the moneys of producers as perfect substitutes. According to this wisdom, coordination among the individual producers is needed to overcome the problem. In other words, a producer cartel is required.

On the other hand, the micro model reverses the implications of the standard approach. Independent adjustment by reserve banks generates lower profit margins, lower costs to holders of reserve bank money, and a higher level of aggregate *real* balances. According to the micro model, therefore, the problem of high holding cost arises only under cartel conditions.

To more thoroughly investigate the differences between the conventional and micro approaches, start by defining a unified monetary system as one consisting of multiple moneys trading at fixed rates of exchange with all other moneys in the system. Leaving the policy objective of money producers unspecified, conventional analysis (Kareken and Wallace, 1981; King, Wallace, and Weber, 1992) concludes that the unified system is consistent with deflation, inflation, or even hyperinflation. In other words, the money and inflation time path is indeterminate.

One variant of the conventional analysis (Rolnick and Weber, 1989; Rolnick, Smith, and Weber, 1993, 1994) attributes a particular objective function – seigniorage maximization – to the money producers in the system. A seigniorage maximizer does not take into account a spill over effect that arises because independent production raises systemwide inflation and reduces the aggregate demand for money and not just the demand for that producer's output. This spill over effect leads to an inflationary bias. The greater the competition, the greater the bias. With perfect competition and zero production costs, money supplies will be increased without limit and the general price level will be undefined (Friedman, 1959). The policy implication is that spill over effects could be internalized by a monopoly producer or a cartel of the multiple producers (Rolnick and Weber, 1989). A more extreme solution would be to require producers to convert their moneys into a real asset, like gold, upon demand.

Rolnick and Weber (1989) use the Federal Reserve System as an example of a unified monetary system that is prone to the seigniorage incentive problem. First, they pose the question: "In what sense . . . does the United States have something other than a single currency?" Their answer is that each note issued clearly shows the Federal Reserve district of origin. "Granted, these differences among Federal Reserve notes are much less distinct than those between, say, US and Italian currencies. Nevertheless, in a physical sense, US currency is not strictly uniform" (1989, pp. 11–12). Second, Rolnick and Weber observe that "the district Federal Reserve banks have an agreement to swap their currencies for any other district's at the fixed rate in any amount and at any time" (1989, p. 12).

Having concluded that the Federal Reserve System is a monetary union, the next step is to indicate that holders of the various Fed notes will tend to treat them as perfect substitutes. As Rolnick, Smith, and Weber note in a more general setting: "The view that in a monetary union with fixed exchange rates, different currencies would be perfect substitutes is motivated by the observation that under such an arrangement all monies have, by definition, the same real rates of return. Consequently, if people choose a currency solely on the basis of its real rate of return, they will view all currencies as the same" (Rolnick, Smith, and Weber, 1993, p. 7).

The final step which triggers the seigniorage incentive problem is that holders of a reserve bank's money are unable to convert it into the dominant money (specie) of the economy. Convertibility is a problem either when reserve banks fail to offer a redemption option or when they make a nominal offer but render it ineffective by providing too few redemption offices or offices in remote locations. Ineffective redemption implies discretionary money issue; discretion which will be used to over issue money (see Selgin and White, 1994).

For good reason, Rolnick and Weber view the modern Federal Reserve as lacking an effective redemption option. After all, since 1971 the gold backing of the Fed's monetary liabilities has been set to zero by law. The Fed has been able to avoid the seigniorage incentive problem only because reserve banks have coordinated their actions.

district Fed banks . . . have an agreement on how to set the rate of money growth and how to distribute the resulting seigniorage. Each district bank participates in the policy process (at Federal Open Market Committee meetings), and a unified policy action is carried out for all twelve districts. No individual district bank can pursue its own monetary policy. Furthermore, all seigniorage is pooled and disbursed by the US Treasury. That is, by design, no district bank can gain by issuing more of its notes than another. Even if all notes were issued by, say, the Ninth District, the revenue would still be pooled and disbursed by the centralized authority (the Treasury).   (Rolnick and Weber, 1989, pp. 12–13)

The bottom line is that over issue of Fed notes (or more generally, Fed money) has been forestalled because monetary policy is centralized. It has not been left to the discretion of individual reserve banks.

The alternative microeconomics interpretation challenges the conclusion that a cartel among reserve banks is required to internalize spill over effects. The legal structure supporting the reserve industry is assumed to be like that characterizing the pre-modern Fed; that is, one that does not proscribe gold backing of money. In this setting, the basic point of contention between the conventional and micro views centers on the breadth of competition. Following a tradition with classical roots (see Glasner, 1985), the micro approach would argue that reserve banks in a decentralized monetary union have opportunities to compete along a number of dimensions. These opportunities include a commitment to redeem their monetary liabilities into specie and to make pecuniary interest payments on their moneys.

But what if these avenues are cut-off as implicitly assumed by the conventional view? Then, borrowing insights from the microeconomics literature, one would expect that producers would compete along some other margin, for instance by offering in-kind payments (free transaction services) to the holders of their moneys. As pointed out in the next section, in-kind payments may be particularly important in the absence of a low cost redemption option. The micro model concludes that independent adjustment results in a seigniorage incentive problem only if *all* competitive margins of adjustment are closed off by legal restrictions.

5.3 Breadth of reserve bank competition after WWI

As far as the Federal Reserve System is concerned, the critical questions in the debate between the conventional and micro views are "do holders of reserve bank money have an effective redemption option?" and "do reserve banks compete with each other by paying interest on their money?" The Federal Reserve Act contained provisions pertaining to both issues. With respect to redemption, section 16 of the Act required that the notes of each reserve bank "shall be redeemed in gold on demand at the Treasury Department of the United States, in the city of Washington, District of Columbia, or in gold or lawful money at the Federal reserve bank."

Because of their focus on the modern Fed, Rolnick and Weber (1989) did not directly address the issue of whether this Federal Reserve Act provision was in fact effective. Rolnick, Smith, and Weber (1994), however, list a number of factors including inconveniently located redemption offices which they perceived as rendering the redemption option ineffective for holders of bank notes before the Fed. Their analysis of pre-Fed banking institutions suggests that they would be hesitant to embrace the notion that section 16 of the Federal Reserve Act provided an effective redemption option.

Selgin and White (1994) directly attack the notion that the Federal Reserve Act provided effective redemption. Indeed, they argue that "The Federal Reserve System provided even less adequately than the National Banking System had for active note redemption" (1994, p. 241). Most important was "a rule preventing a bank from directly receiving reserve-balance credit from its district reserve bank for a deposit of notes issued in other districts. Member banks were thus encouraged to return their own reserve bank's notes, but not to send in the notes issued by other district reserve banks" (1994, p. 242). Selgin and White conclude that in both the National Bank System and the Federal Reserve System "interventions of the federal government prevented the stock of bank notes from adjusting in an automatic and desirable way, in response to changes in the demand to hold notes" (1994, p. 243).

Selgin and White's conclusions that redemption was not an effective option under the Federal Reserve Act and that Fed money did not automatically adjust are not completely convincing. Indeed, the previous chapter documented the "automatic and desirable" adjustment in bank reserves on a seasonal basis in the 1920s. Moreover, the source – a 1914 paper by economist F. M. Taylor – on which Selgin and White most heavily rely comes down on the side of "automatic and desirable" adjustment in Fed notes. In his paper titled "The elasticity of note issue under the new currency law," Taylor reviews both sides of the argument and concludes that "when we take the new law as a whole, it seems not unreasonable to affirm that it promises to accomplish, directly or indirectly, most of the ends which we had hoped to attain through elasticity and hence promises to give us a system which in essentials is truly and adequately elastic" (1914, p. 463).

The key here is to appreciate the "promise" referred to in the quotation from Taylor. To be sure, reserve banks did not provide an elastic money when they opened for business in November 1914. But inelasticity was not due to the absence of redemption options. It was due to the straitjacket imposed initially by the holding of a 100 percent specie reserve and later by the wartime financing policy (see chapter 3). Once the straitjacket was removed after World War I, an elastic money could become more than just a "promise."

Even if the holders of reserve money are able to surmount the types of redemption obstacles cited by Rolnick, Smith, and Weber (1994) and by Selgin and White (1994), it is important to recognize that redemption does not eliminate but merely reduces the seigniorage incentive problem. At most section 16 of the Act guarantees the prospective holder of a reserve bank dollar, who may have paid gold to obtain the dollar, a real holding return of zero. This is a sub-competitive real return which provides reserve banks with a monopolistic profit margin and, according to conventional wisdom, some incentive to expand money issue beyond the optimal level. Elimination of the seigniorage incentive problem requires a market structure that induces reserve banks to pay competitive returns on reserve bank money, perhaps in the form of explicit monetary interest payments or equivalently a below-par acquisition price for a note.

Several attributes of the new Fed System made elimination of the seigniorage incentive problem less than straightforward. First, the par pricing provisions of the Act restricted reserve banks from offering their notes at a price below face value in order to attract business. Second, while the Act did not expressly prohibit the payment of monetary interest on reserves, the example set by European central banks weighed against such payments (Conway, 1914, p. 324). Third, the Act's redemption guarantee was subject to a time consistency problem. Future legislators might pass amendments to the original act nullifying redemption, or future Fed decision makers might shirk in enforcing the guarantee.

As was pointed out in chapter 4, however, there was one key feature of the Federal Reserve Act which bolsters the micro view's position. Section 17 called upon reserve banks to provide check-clearing and currency services for member banks with the service fees to be set by the Federal Reserve Board. By 1918 the Board had established a zero pricing policy which implied that the real value of services represented a real interest payment on reserves. Importantly, a commitment by a reserve bank management team to pay interest through in-kind payments could not easily be overturned by another management team in the future. The reason is that the provision of check-clearing and currency services generally entails an irreversible capital expenditure. Once the investment is made, holders of reserve bank money are guaranteed a minimum real rate of return. Moreover, this minimum real rate of return could be supplemented by the already mentioned provision in the Federal Reserve Act which authorized reserve banks to offer discount loans at rates of discount subject to "review and determination" by the Board. If the discount rate is set below market levels, then the real return on reserves is higher than the minimum guaranteed return.

The upshot is that the Federal Reserve Act provided a solution to the seigniorage incentive problem that, arguably, was superior to a simple specie redemption guarantee. At best, an unqualified redemption option promises a real return of zero while the in-kind payment, and the underlying capital expenditure, guarantees a real rate of return greater than zero. The magnitude of this real return would depend on the market structure of the System. If reserve banks were able to form an effective cartel, then the real rate of return would be relatively modest. The cartel solution depends, of course, on the existence of some mechanism for detecting and punishing reserve banks which attempt to independently adjust. The next section considers the circumstances under which reserve banks will have an incentive to use open market operations to break the cartel and how independent adjustment tends to bid up the real rate of return on Fed money.

5.4 Modeling competitive open market operations

With respect to the postwar period, there are several points of contention between the conventional and micro views. First, what constitutes the appropriate measure of the opportunity cost of holding reserve bank money? Second, how does competition affect the holding cost? Third, and most important, do competitive open market operations lead to an over issue of Fed money?

The conventional analysis argues that reserve banks do not pay interest on money, either explicitly or implicitly. Moreover, the conventional view in its strongest form would question the effectiveness of the gold redemption clause in the Federal Reserve Act. The upshot is that aggregate nominal money production controls the nominal loan rate and this rate represents the opportunity cost of holding money. Competitive pressures induce reserve banks to conduct open market operations for earnings which leads to an over issue of nominal money. Market loan rates increase, reserve holding costs increase, and the real amount of money demanded falls.

The micro model challenges the conventional conclusions. Gold redemption is an effective option that pegs the general price level and inflation. Under these circumstances, the loan rate is not endogenous to the reserve industry. Nor is it the true holding cost measure since competitive pressures would induce reserve banks to pay interest on reserves. The competitive equilibrium is one where reserve holding costs are low, inducing banks to hold relatively large amounts of nominal and real Fed money.

To formally indicate how competitive open market operations affect holding costs in the micro model, start with the set-up from chapters 2 and 3. In that basic set-up, reserve banks offered only discount loans at a rate established by the Board. They did not attempt to supplement loans with open market operations. An important result of this section is that the domination of discount loans in the portfolios of reserve banks cannot be taken for granted; that is, it is not a necessary condition of equilibrium. Whether or not discount loans dominate, turns out to be dependent on the relationship between discount rates and market interest rates. If at any time the discount rate is a penalty rate, then a profit opportunity arises for independent open market operations.

Introducing open market operations into the model requires a separation of total reserves into borrowed and non-borrowed components. Recall from chapters 2 and 3 that the holding cost associated with discount loans was $c^B = [i\rho + d(1-\rho) - r]$, with the superscript, B, signifying borrowed reserves. Open market operations will produce non-borrowed (NB) reserves with a holding cost of simply $c^{NB} = (i - r)$. The non-borrowed holding cost is related to the borrowed holding cost by the equation $c^{NB} = c^B + (i-d)(1-\rho)$. The spread between c^{NB} and c^B equals $(i-d)(1-\rho)$ which depends on values for i, d and ρ. Continue to assume that the discount rate is set by the central administrative unit, the Board, that the market interest rate is determined in a worldwide market, and that the gold reserve ratio is determined by technological factors.

Under what circumstances will individual reserve banks have an incentive to conduct open market operations? The prewar straitjacket outcome of chapter 3 arises when $\rho = 1$ which gives $(i-d)(1-\rho) = 0$. Independent adjustment does not occur in this special case since there is no competitive advantage to be won by a single reserve bank engaging in open market operations.

The wartime preferential discount rate policy implied that the discount rate was a subsidy rate which, in combination with the wartime gold reserve ratio of less than one, gives $(i-d)(1-\rho) > 0$. Because the holding cost of non-borrowed reserves was greater than the cost of borrowed reserves, banks would satisfy their entire demand for reserves by visiting the discount window and paying the cost set by the Board. While a reserve bank would like to produce more money by conducting open market operations, it is unable to do so because member banks refuse to pay the relatively high holding cost associated with the extra production. Once again, independent adjustment does not occur.

The interesting case arose after the war on those occasions when the discount rate was a penalty rate. Because the gold reserve ratio was below one throughout the twenties, a penalty discount rate would imply that $(i-d)(1-\rho) < 0$ and banks would prefer non-borrowed reserves. Figure 5.1 depicts this case. Position B indicates the reference solution with the Board implementing a discount policy which, in the absence of independent adjustment, would generate monopolistic rents for reserve banks. But with $d > i$, reserve banks have an opportunity to supply reserves at the per unit holding cost c^{NB} which is lower than c^B by the amount $(i-d)(1-\rho)$. For reserve banks acting jointly this would not be a winning proposition since it moves the System away from the cartel solution. For a reserve bank acting independently, however, open market operations provide a contingent profit opportunity.

Designate $[-(i-d)(1-\rho)]$ as the chiseling spread. The greater the chiseling spread, the greater the return to independent adjustment. If the discount

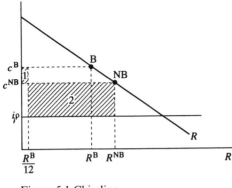

Figure 5.1 Chiseling

committee is unable to control market shares, then a reserve bank acting independently could use open market operations to capture the entire market. The total potential gain to chiseling equals the difference between area 2 in the figure and area 1. When all reserve banks independently adjust, the solution will be at NB. In moving from B to NB, non-borrowed reserves will have displaced borrowed reserves with total reserves now somewhat higher.

A special case of interest is where the chiseling spread is only slightly greater than zero. In figure 5.1, NB would be just to the right of B on the demand curve and competition would not significantly affect the holding cost. Open market operations have no monetary policy implications in that the displacement of non-borrowed reserves for borrowed reserves is one-for-one. Chapter 6 highlights this result and refers to it as the scissors effect.

To summarize, only when the discount rate is a penalty rate will the chiseling spread be positive providing reserve banks with a seigniorage incentive to conduct open market operations. In contrast to the conventional view, competitive open market operations do not result in a "tragedy of the commons" type outcome with skyrocketing holding costs. Competition in the reserve market operates as in ordinary markets: price (holding cost) falls.

5.5 Empirical overview

In assessing whether the micro model provides insights into the operation of the Fed, consider figures 5.2 and 5.3. Figure 5.2 shows the two major earning assets of the reserve banks, discount loans and government securities, and figure 5.3 shows the chiseling spread from the middle of 1917 to 1924.[1] The preferential rate policy during the war resulted in a negative chiseling spread so that discount loans were the preferred earning asset of

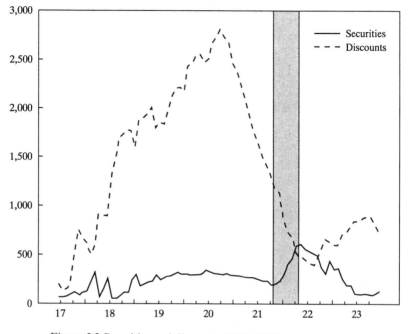

Figure 5.2 Securities and discounts, 1917–1923

reserve banks. The huge wartime increase in Fed credit can be attributed to member bank borrowing.

The shaded area in the two figures indicates the postwar competitive period. In figure 5.2, government security holdings of reserve banks rose from about $150 million to $600 million. According to the micro model, the switch from discount loans to government securities would have occurred only if the chiseling spread had increased. Two factors contributed to this result. First, the preferential rate policy was phased out at the end of 1921. Second, declining market interest rates in the aftermath of the war (with discontinuous adjustment in the discount rate) tended to produce a continuous increase in the spread. Figure 5.3 shows that the chiseling spread rose throughout the period, crossing from negative to positive at mid point. A local maximum was achieved at the end of the competitive period.

The micro model implies that the competitive open market operations accompanying the positive chiseling spread would be detrimental to systemwide profits and would prompt a cartel-like response. This is precisely what occurred. In an effort to reassert central control over open market operations, reserve banks formed a Committee of Governors on Central Execution of Purchases and Sales of Government Securities by

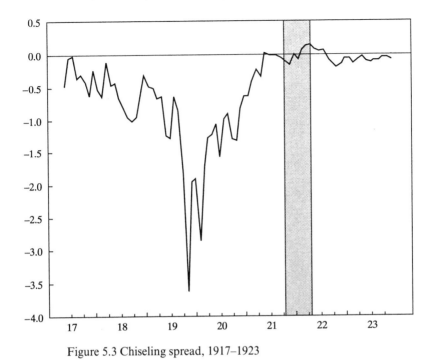

Figure 5.3 Chiseling spread, 1917–1923

Federal Reserve banks in May 1922. The committee recommended gradual liquidation of government security holdings and throughout the rest of 1922 the proportion of the System's earning assets held as government securities declined (see figure 5.2). The liquidation policy continued into the new year. At this time, however, several reserve banks again purchased securities for their own account. A new committee, the Open Market Investment Committee, with stronger enforcement powers replaced the old one in April 1923 and liquidation resumed. At the end of the year a Special System Investment Account was established at the New York Federal Reserve which served as the joint account for dealing in government securities on behalf of all the reserve banks.

What is really at issue in the debate between the conventional and micro views is the behaviour of *aggregate* Fed credit. The proponents of the over issue hypothesis must argue that the surge in security holdings during the competitive period would lead to a significant increase in Fed credit. Only after the open market operation committee formed in May 1922 would Fed credit reverse course. In contrast, the micro view rejects the prediction of over issue during the competitive period. Moreover, because the chiseling spread moved within a relatively tight band from the end of 1921 to 1924 the

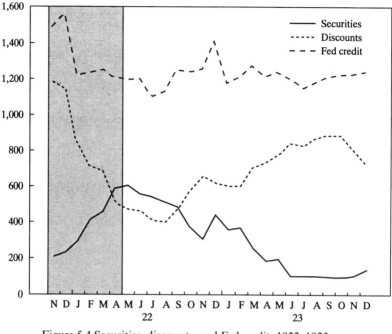

Figure 5.4 Securities, discounts, and Fed credit, 1922–1923

micro model would predict that total Fed credit would also move within a relatively tight band. Figure 5.4 confirms this implication. Total Fed credit was relatively smooth because changes in government security holdings were offset by changes in discount loans.

5.6 Conclusion

The contribution of this chapter has been to analyze a historical episode to determine whether competition among money producers, given certain preconditions, generates outcomes similar to the outcomes generated in other competitive markets. The important precondition is that money producers be allowed to compete along some price dimension. This condition was satisfied for the Federal Reserve System in the immediate aftermath (1921–3) of World War I. Contrary to conventional wisdom, competition among the 12 reserve banks did not give rise to a seigniorage incentive problem.

For the most part, economic historians have regarded the 1921–3 period as a transition period during which Fed officials developed the techniques necessary to control reserve bank competition (Chandler, 1958, p. 233). According to this view, the independent adjustment problem was solved by

1924 and the economic stability over the next few years, 1924–8, was due to the open market policy skills of Federal Reserve officials. Indeed, Friedman and Schwartz (1963, chapter 6) claim that this period represented "the high tide of the Federal Reserve System."

The microeconomics approach would suggest more scepticism. After all, the open market coordination that developed during the 1920s was not backed by a permanent, legally sanctioned enforcement mechanism and therefore would be susceptible to attack. The micro view would point to the fact that the 1921–2 increase in open market operations was not atypical. As I point out in the next chapter, there was an increase of similar magnitude in 1924. While the conventional view would tend to interpret the decade of the twenties as one of successful coordination interrupted by one exceptional episode of independent adjustment, a hard-nosed micro view would tend to interpret the period as one of reserve bank competition interrupted by occasional episodes of coordination.

At a more fundamental level, the two views differ in their interpretation of the Fed's ability to control the money supply. Presumably, the conventional view that centralized open market operations were responsible for economic stability in the mid and late 1920s rests on the notion that these operations control aggregate Fed money. On the other hand, if open market operations simply displace discount loans, then the Fed is unable to control the money supply much less movements in the total output of the economy.

Interestingly, this displacement effect has generally been regarded by macroeconomic historians as a defining feature of 1920s monetary policy. For obvious reasons, it has been labelled the scissors effect (for example, see Friedman and Schwartz, 1963, chapter 6). Evidence presented in this chapter suggests that the displacement of discount loans by open market operations was approximately one-for-one in the period from 1921 to 1923. The next chapter attempts to provide a precise measure of the so-called scissors effect for the entire decade of the twenties as a means of providing additional evidence on the predictive power of the micro model and on the more general issue of how much of the seeming stability of the period from 1924 to 1928 can be attributed to a centralized policy orchestrated by the Federal Reserve.

6   High tide of the Federal Reserve System?

6.1. Introduction

Economic historians tend to view the 1920s as a period when the Federal Reserve System actively used open market operations as an effective policy tool. In chapter 6 of *A Monetary History of the US, 1867–1960* Milton Friedman and Anna Schwartz refer to this period as the "high tide of the Federal Reserve System." During the twenties there

> was a conscious attempt, for perhaps the first time in monetary history, to use central-bank powers to promote internal economic stability as well as to preserve balance in international payments and to prevent and moderate strictly financial crises. In retrospect, we can see that this was a major step toward the assumption by government of explicit continuous responsibility for economic stability. As the decade wore on, the System took – and perhaps even more was given – credit for the generally stable conditions that prevailed, and high hopes were placed in the potency of monetary policy as then administered. (1963, p. 240)

According to Friedman and Schwartz, and other high tide proponents, the ability and willingness of the System to conduct stabilization policy was enhanced by the gradual centralization of open market operations which culminated in the creation of an Open Market Investment Committee in 1923. The centralization of authority allowed the Fed to manipulate Federal Reserve credit to offset secular shocks to the economy and to eliminate seasonal movements in interest rates (Friedman and Schwartz, 1963, pp. 292–8; Miron, 1986).

Friedman and Schwartz's characterization of the 1920s Fed as an adept benevolent stabilizer seems strangely out of place with their discussion of the rest of Fed history. Instead of the benevolent stabilizer motif, they occasionally portrayed reserve banks as self-interested bureaucracies which built-up their security portfolios for earning purposes (see previous chapter), or more frequently as automaton-like decision makers subservient to the Treasury (Friedman and Schwartz, 1963, chapters 9 and 10). But the most striking departure from the twenties high tide theme emerges in Friedman and Schwartz's Great Depression chapter that concludes with the subsection – "Why was monetary policy so inept?" In moving from the late twenties to the early thirties, Fed officials suddenly were transformed from adroit fine tuners to ill-informed de-stabilizers.

How do Friedman and Schwartz explain the exceptional record of the Fed during the 1920s, given its unwillingness or inability to pursue stabilization policy during the rest of its existence? In the high tide chapter, they resort to "accidental event" and "personality" (1963, pp. 411–19) explanations. Before accepting these explanations, the factual basis of the Friedman and Schwartz claim that policy was uniquely effective during the 1920s must be established.

The Friedman and Schwartz claim can be challenged at two levels. First, the micro model's implication that open market operations result in a displacement (scissors) effect can be used to challenge the claim that the Fed was able to use open market operations to control Federal Reserve credit. Second, a finding that the Fed does not control its credit challenges the notion that the Fed was responsible for stabilizing the economy by eliminating seasonal fluctuations in interest rates.

6.2 Scissors effect

High tide economists do not deny that open market operations may cause banks to visit the discount window. Friedman and Schwartz explicitly acknowledge this possibility in their discussion of the Board's *Tenth Annual Report* for 1923. The report

demonstrates, on the basis of experience during 1922 and 1923, the tendency of open market purchases to reduce the volume of discounting and open market sales to increase it – the so-called scissors effect. This was the first explicit recognition of the coordinate importance of open market operations and rediscounting for general credit policy. . . . The report provides a rationalization for the open market committee, which had been tentatively organized in 1922, and reorganized in 1923, after purchases by individual Banks to obtain earnings had demonstrated both the general credit effects of such purchases and the need for coordination.

(Friedman and Schwartz, 1963, p. 251)

According to Friedman and Schwartz, monetary policy during 1924 was a prime example of successful coordination, at least in the view of interested parties at the time.

The Reserve System's holdings of government securities were increased from a low of $73 million in November 1923 to $588 million a year later, the greater part of the increase taking place in the seven months from February to September 1924. Federal Reserve credit reached a trough in June 1924; and total high-powered money resumed its earlier rate of growth. The trough of the recession is dated in July 1924.

It is by no means clear how to interpret the close synchronism of Reserve action and business movements during that episode. Doubtless there were effects both ways and common causes as well. But there seems little doubt that the synchronism impressed itself strongly on contemporaries, both inside and outside the System, and strengthened the confidence of both groups in the potency of Reserve System powers. The episode almost surely played an important role in the development of the policy statement in the 1923 report.   (Friedman and Schwartz, 1963, p. 288)

The general picture which emerges from this account is that by 1924 the System was aware of the propensity of open market purchases to reduce bank borrowing and it used this knowledge to manipulate total Fed credit for economic stability purposes. Implicit in this view is the presumption that the scissors effect was partial. Under these circumstances, the Fed could use open market operations to control its credit, as well as reserves and high-powered money.

An alternative view of Fed policy in 1924 is based on a study originally prepared in 1971 by D'Arista, Staff Member, House Committee on Banking and Currency. The study used stenographic records of Fed meetings and conferences not previously available to researchers. D'Arista (1994) indicates that while the open market committee nominally controlled open market operations in 1924, the competitive forces which were operative early on in 1922 also were operative in 1924. The superficial difference was that in 1922 individual reserve banks conducted their own open market operations whereas in 1924 a central committee, *faced with repeated threats of independent adjustment by the individual reserve banks*, conducted policy. At a fundamental level open market operations in both cases were driven by individual reserve bank earning considerations rather than general credit policy considerations.

D'Arista documents in some detail how earning considerations and the threat of independent adjustment influenced the policy of the 1924 Conference of Governors and the open market committee.

At the beginning of January 1924, the committee recommended purchases of $15 million. On January 12, Randolph Burgess, then an official of the New York bank, sent a memorandum to Deputy Governor Case warning that if the current policy "toward reduction of the earning assets of the System" were continued, the earnings position of the Reserve banks would become serious unless business picked up. The committee prepared a statement indicating that, as of January 30, the System's earnings were at the lowest point since November 1917. Anticipating pressure from the Reserve banks for individual purchases, the committee revised its allotment plan to make the need for earnings, rather than the reserve positions of various banks, the basis for distributing assets. . . . The effect was to delay the commencement of substantial purchases by the System for several months. . . . As it was, the system did not make substantial purchases until April.

. . . the system was still short $18 million of earning assets to cover estimated expenses for 1924 even after the substantial purchases in April that had been approved by the board. The conference voted to increase the system account by purchases of an additional $150 million of government securities and adopted a new plan of allotment based on earnings requirements. . . . This did not solve the problem, however, and in June both the Chicago and the Philadelphia banks threatened to make substantial individual purchases to meet expenses. Therefore, the committee voted on July 1, 1924, to increase system holdings by another $100 million.

(D'Arista, 1994, pp. 128–30)

According to D'Arista, the open market committee produced the type of outcome that would have been produced by individual reserve banks acting on their own; at best, the committee succeeded in delaying the independent adjustment outcome by a few months.

Although the high tide and competitive views agree that there was a high degree of "synchronism of Reserve action and business movements" they would differ in their interpretation of what this implied about the effectiveness of policy. For the most part the high tide view is that Fed actions were coordinated and effective. Open market operations led to an increase in total Fed credit and forestalled recessionary tendencies in the economy. The micro view reverses the direction of causation and calls attention to the scissors effect. The recession of 1924, by depressing interest rates, tended to foster competitive open market operations but these operations did not result in an increase in total Fed credit. Policy was rendered ineffective by a complete scissors effect. Summing up, in one view Fed actions showed the "potency of Reserve System powers" and in the other they reflected the "pressure from individual purchases."

Figures 6.1 and 6.2 provide the basis for a preliminary assessment of the micro view. The shaded areas indicate the two episodes of competition, 1921/2 and 1924, as defined by the descriptive accounts of D'Arista. The pattern of chiseling rates in each episode is consistent with the micro view. As indicated in the previous chapter, rates rose throughout the first episode, crossing from negative to positive approximately midway. In the second episode, rates were positive throughout reaching a high near the end. As for the composition of earning assets, government securities displaced discount loans in both episodes. There is no evidence supporting the conventional concern that competition would lead to "easy money." Total Fed credit fell during the first few months of the initial episode (as it had done throughout the postwar) and then leveled off. During the second episode, total Fed credit at first fell and then rose.

Although the 1924 episode (along with the 1921/2 episode) perhaps best illustrates the tension between conventional and micro views, the two views also differ in their interpretation of monetary policy over the remainder of

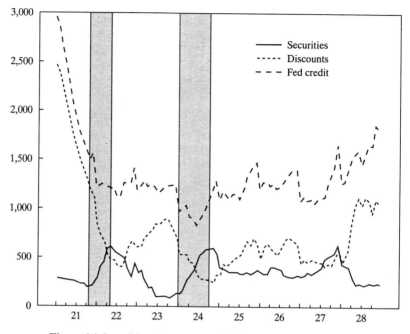

Figure 6.1 Securities, discounts, and Fed credit, 1921–1928

the decade. In particular, the micro view would call attention to the fact that the chiseling spread (see figure 6.2) was sometimes positive and sometimes negative but, at least until 1928, it fluctuated within a relatively narrow band of (-0.5) to (0.25). Therefore, the micro view would predict that total Fed credit would fluctuate within a relatively narrow band, with government securities displacing discount loans on an approximately one-for-one basis during periods when the chiseling spread was above zero and with discount loans displacing government securities on an approximately one-for-one basis during periods when the chiseling spread was below zero. The smoothness in Fed credit from 1922 to 1927 in figure 6.1 is indicative of a one-for-one offset.

The sharp increase in discount loans in 1928 corresponded to a sharp drop in the chiseling spread in figure 6.2. But why the sharp increase in total Fed credit? Why, in other words, was the increase in discount loans accompanied by a less than one-for-one drop in government securities. This result would be consistent with the micro view if the demand for Fed credit was rising. The fact that the economy was expanding in 1928 would tend to produce this demand shift.

A 1989 study of mine (Toma, 1989) more formally tested for the scissors

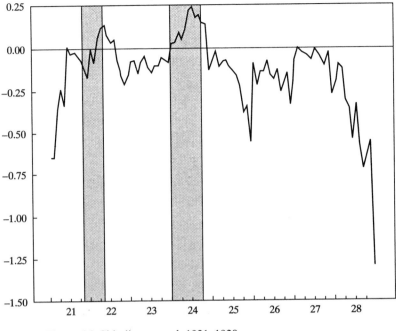

Figure 6.2 Chiseling spread, 1921–1928

effect during the 1920s. The test period was for 1924–9. Using monthly data, I regressed the first difference of the Fed's government security holdings (OMO) against lagged first differences of securities and lagged first differences of Fed discounts (DIS).[1]

The results are reported in column 1 of table 6.1. Lagged values of Fed government security holdings are jointly significant in explaining member bank discounting. For the period from 1924 to 1929 the hypothesis that open market operations do not affect (Granger-cause) discounting can be rejected at the 0.003 significance level. Moreover, the coefficients on the security variables imply a certain pattern of bank discounting over time in reaction to open market operations. For example a one-dollar security purchase in the current month is associated with a 59 cent drop in discounting the next month and another 61 cent drop in the month thereafter. Ignoring significance levels, and simply adding together all the security coefficients, implies a 97 cent decrease in discounting after five months. An F-test indicates that this sum is not significantly different from minus one. The simple version of the micro hypothesis cannot be rejected: an injection of reserves into the banking system in the current month leads to a decrease in bank discounting which offsets the original injection exactly.

Table 6.1 *Scissors effect tests*

$$\text{DIS}_t = a + \sum_{i=1}^{r} b_i \, \text{DIS}_{t-i} + \sum_{j=1}^{s} c_j \, \text{OMO}_{t-j} + e_t$$

Independent variables	1924–9 [r=3, s=5] (1)	1922–9 [r=3, s=2] (2)
Constant	3.14 (10.52)	−3.60 (9.05)
DIS_{t-1}	−0.16 (0.13)	−0.08 (0.11)
DIS_{t-2}	−0.22 (0.13)	−0.14 (0.11)
DIS_{t-3}	0.15 (0.14)	0.23 (0.11)
OMO_{t-1}	−0.59 (0.23)	−0.49 (0.18)
OMO_{t-2}	−0.61 (0.25)	−0.46 (0.19)
OMO_{t-3}	−0.32 (0.26)	
OMO_{t-4}	−0.06 (0.27)	
OMO_{t-5}	0.61 (0.24)	
R^2	0.31	0.23
F-stat/prob > F (all c_j=0)	4.08/0.003	6.51/0.002
F-stat/prob > F (sum c_j=-1)	0.00/0.950	0.04/0.852

Note: Standard errors in parentheses to right of coefficient values.

Column 2 extends the sample period back to 1922. The results generally are consistent with those reported in column 1. For the 1922–9 period, there is a 95 cent decrease in discounting after two months.

Overall, the table provides strong evidence against the high tide view that the Fed of the 1920s discovered how to use open market policy to fine tune the economy. More to the point, the evidence indicates that the Fed did not have any such stabilization powers. The private banking system reacted to open market operations in a way that eliminated any lasting effect these operations might have had on Federal Reserve credit. At least with respect to open market operations, Friedman and Schwartz's high tide label appears inappropriate.

6.3 Seasonal movements in Federal Reserve credit and interest rates

The finding that centralized open market operations did not control Fed credit casts doubt upon the related high tide hypothesis that the Fed used open market operations during the 1920s to smooth interest rates. Table 6.2 presents the results of testing for seasonality in both Fed credit and the call rate of interest over various sub-periods before and after the Fed's creation.

Table 6.2 *Tests for seasonal movement in monthly growth rate of Fed credit and monthly change in the call rate*

| Period (1) | Fed credit | | Call rate | |
	F (2)	Q (3)	F (4)	Q (5)
1890-1914	—	—	5.13 (0.0001)	20.47*
1915–40	5.39 (0.0001)	65.42*	2.31 (0.01)	11.84*
1915–21	0.66 (0.77)	2.12	1.89 (0.05)	4.23
1918–21	0.77 (0.67)	1.11	1.90 (0.07)	1.83
1922–8	23.01 (0.0001)	69.80*	3.56 (0.0005)	11.58*
1929–33	1.92 (0.06)	2.26	1.20 (0.31)	0.00

Notes:
Significance level is in parentheses. *Exceeds 0.05 critical value.
Source: Board of Governors, *Banking and Monetary Statistics* (1943).

The F-statistics are computed by regressing the first difference of the log of Fed credit and the first difference of the call rate on a set of 12 monthly dummies (with no intercept) and then testing whether the last 11 dummy coefficients jointly differ from the first. For the Q-statistics, the procedure is to estimate the first three (positive) annual autocorrelation coefficients of the first difference of the log of Fed credit and the call rate and then multiply the number of months in the sample period by the sum of the squared values of the coefficients.

The summary statistics for the two long periods, 1890–1914 and 1915–40, indicate less seasonality of interest rates for the latter period, though seasonality is statistically significant for both periods. Breaking the data into sub-periods, however, is more revealing. During the period 1915–21, the seasonality of the call rate is less pronounced than in the period before creation of the Fed, 1890–1914. During the same period, however, the table suggests that Federal Reserve credit is not significantly higher during the fall (also see Clark, 1986). Miron (1986, p. 133) claims that before 1918 "the problems of financing World War I constrained its [the Fed's] ability to conduct discretionary open market operations." After excluding the war years and focusing on the period 1918–21, however, there still is no evidence of significant seasonality of Fed credit, but this may be due in part to the small sample size. A closer examination of the data reveals only one year, 1919, in which the growth of Fed credit is much higher for the last part of the year than for the rest of the year. That is also the only year in which the call rate of interest is much higher late in the year.

For the period 1922–8, monthly Fed credit displays significant seasonality which confirms Miron's results for weekly data. Seasonality of the call rate, however, is greater than during the 1915–21 period. The seasonal patterns in Fed credit and the call rate from 1922 to 1928 (not shown) are similar; both tend to be higher during the fall. A plot of the monthly first differences of each variable (not shown) indicates that those years with a particularly large increase in Fed credit during the fall (for instance, 1924 and 1927) also tend to be years with particularly large fall increases in the call rate. More formally, comparing the difference between the mean growth rate of Fed credit during the last five months of each year and the mean growth rate for the entire year with a similar measure of seasonality for the call rate gives a correlation coefficient of 0.75 (significant at the 0.05 level).

Further testing (see Holland and Toma, 1991) points to the source of the seasonal behavior of Fed credit. Both bankers' acceptances purchased and discount loans displayed significant seasonality during the period 1922–8 but not during the period 1915–21. Fed holdings of government securities, on the other hand, were not close to displaying significant seasonality in either sub-period, especially 1922–8. This indicates that the overall seasonal behavior of Fed credit during 1922–8 was driven by the demands of the private banking system rather than by the Fed's open market operation policy.

6.4 The Great Depression

A final issue concerns the reappearance of financial panics during the Great Depression. The first shock to the economic system occurred in October 1929 with the stock market crash and was followed by the first banking crisis which lasted from October 1930 to January 1931. Two other crises occurred with the last ending with the March 1933 banking holiday.

The conventional view as represented by Miron focuses on the fact that there seemed to be a change in the seasonal fluctuation in Fed credit beginning in 1929 (Miron, 1986, pp. 136–7). Fed credit failed to expand at the end of the year as it typically had during the 1920s.[2] According to Miron the absence of a seasonal Fed credit policy would naturally cause interest rates to become seasonal once again, making the banking system susceptible to a

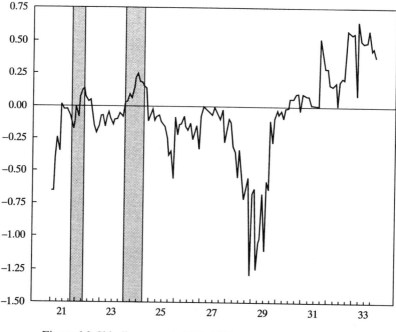

Figure 6.3 Chiseling spread, 1921–1933

crisis once again. Table 6.2, however, points to a problem with this view: the reduced seasonal fluctuation of Fed credit for 1929–33 did not increase the seasonal fluctuation of interest rates.

The micro model, with its emphasis on implicit interest payments, offers a different explanation of the re-emergence of the financial crisis problem. The banking system would again become susceptible to unexpected shocks if (1) the Board effectively shut down the discount window by raising the discount rate above market rates; in other words, by raising the chiseling spread from negative to positive and (2) an open market operation cartel eliminated individual reserve bank chiseling. The first policy would not only reduce borrowed reserves but in addition would make *routine* end-of-the-year implicit interest payments no longer available through the Federal Reserve's discount window. The second policy would preclude the type of independent adjustment that occurred during the 1920s when the chiseling rate occasionally was positive. With an effective open market operation cartel, reserve banks could not fill in the void left by the decrease in borrowed reserves by acquiring government securities for their own account.

Figure 6.3 extends the chiseling spread from figure 6.2 into the depression years, 1929–33. The figure shows a dramatic change in the chiseling spread in 1929. For the most part, the change was due to a change in discount policy; that is, a change in the spread between the call rate and the discount rate. The discount subsidy reached a local high of 4.23 in July 1929, dropped to 2.23 in the next month and to 0.43 in October. Figure 6.3 shows that the chiseling spread rose from around -1 to around -0.25. By July 1930 the chiseling spread had turned positive for the first time since 1924. Except for one month, the spread did not drop below zero for the rest of the depression. The change in the spread from consistently negative to consistently positive represented an end to the Board's policy in the mid twenties of an "open" discount window and therefore a curtailment of the preventative policy of providing routine end of the year subsidies to the private banking system.

A positive chiseling spread need not pose unusual problems for the financial system. After all, the spread had been positive for parts of 1922 and 1924. These episodes, however, do not provide a guide for what to expect in the 1930s. One difference was that the chiseling spread exceeded zero by a relatively small amount in the first part of 1922 and 1924. At the end of each year, the natural tendency of interest rates to rise somewhat caused the spread to fall to a level below zero. During the early thirties, the spread also fell at years' end. But since the spread was so high at the beginning of the year, the spread remained positive (the discount rate remained at penalty levels) at the end. Thus, end of the year subsidies were no longer provided to the banking system as they had been during the 1922 and 1924 episodes.

A second difference was the degree to which open market operations were centralized. The defining characteristic of the 1922 and 1924 episodes was that the Open Market Investment Committee did not have the power to prevent chiseling. Each reserve bank could conduct open market operations for its own account. The open market mechanism was reorganized, however, in early 1930 when an Open Market Policy Conference replaced the Open Market Investment Committee. The new group included all 12 Reserve bank governors. All open market operations were to be undertaken by the new body with a majority of governors required for a policy change.

Events in 1929 were the proximate cause of this organizational change. In response to the October 1929 stock market crash, the New York Fed purchased $160 million of government securities for its own account.

Members of the Board regarded the New York Bank's failure to seek authorization of the Board before taking action as smacking of insubordination . . . As a legal matter, the New York Bank seemed clearly within its rights. Under the 1923 agreement setting up the Open Market Investment Committee, each Reserve Bank retained the right to purchase and hold government securities for its own account . . . . most Board members acknowledged the legal right yet felt that the challenge to the Board's authority was insupportable.   (Friedman and Schwartz, 1963, p. 364)

The Board suggested that no further purchases of government securities be made except with the approval of the Board.

Later in November Governor Young of the Federal Reserve Board and Harrison, President of the New York Fed, met to discuss open market policy. In that meeting Harrison commented on the Board's position

that we should go to the Federal Reserve Board in advance for prior approval of any transactions in government securities. . . . I told him that the logical consequence of his point of view, which was that the Federal Reserve Board should approve of all these things in advance, was that the Federal Reserve Board would become a central bank operating in Washington. . . . [H]is only comment was that the Federal Reserve Board had been given most extraordinarily wide powers, that as long as the Board had those powers, they would feel free to exercise them and Congress could determine whether they objected to having a central bank operating in Washington.

(Friedman and Schwartz, 1963, p. 365)

The end result of that discussion was that Harrison agreed to refrain from independent open market operations until a more permanent arrangement could be worked out with the Board. The arrangement eventually agreed to was the above-mentioned formation of the Open Market Policy Conference. Under this new structure there was considerable doubt as to whether a reserve bank could independently purchase securities for its own account without receiving prior approval from the Board. This legal uncertainty was sufficient to dissuade the New York Fed from acting independently (Friedman and Schwartz, 1963, pp. 369–74).

The upshot was that the Board exercised considerable power over discount *and* open market operation policy. Whereas a countercyclical open market policy naturally occurred as a result of independent adjustment in the 1920s, now, with the chiseling loophole closed off, an increase in the System's government security holdings would require a policy initiative endorsed by the Board as well as by a majority of the Open Market Policy Conference. The micro model predicts that the new body would have no such incentive. As became apparent in 1930, a countercyclical outcome was not preferred by the Conference.

Prior to the September 25, 1930, meeting of the Open Market Policy Conference, Governor Harrison circulated a proposal advocating countercyclical operations but not involving 'any very large amount' of purchases. In view of Harrison's belief that 'the seriousness of the present depression is so great,' it was a modest proposal. Nevertheless, a majority of the Reserve bank governors opposed it, and it was voted down at the conference. (D'Arista, 1994, p. 160)

Figure 6.4 indicates that the System's security holdings rose in 1930, but not by enough to offset the fall in discount loans that occurred because of the shutting down of the discount window. Substantial open market operations

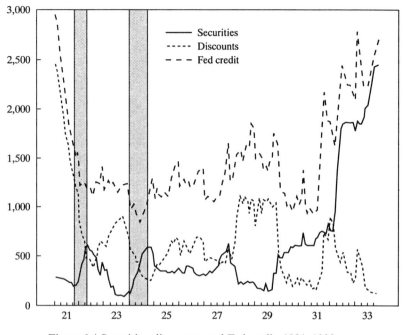

Figure 6.4 Securities, discounts, and Fed credit, 1921–1933

were not undertaken until 1932 and these were made largely in response to congressional pressures (D'Arista, 1994, p. 163; Friedman and Schwartz, 1963, p. 363).

6.5 Conclusion

This chapter has provided evidence on the effect of open market operations on Fed credit (the scissors effect) and the effect of Fed credit on the seasonal fluctuation of interest rates which challenges the conventional view that the 1920s represented the high tide of the Federal Reserve System. With respect to the scissors effect, an open market operations impact on Fed credit tended to be offset one-for-one with a change in member bank discounting. On the basis of this evidence, it is incorrect to view the Fed as a central monetary authority which used open market operations to offset exogenous shocks to the economy. In this sense the "high tide" label is inappropriate.

With respect to the seasonal fluctuation of interest rates, the evidence points to the following. First, there are periods after creation of the Fed when neither Federal Reserve credit nor interest rates exhibit significant seasonal movement. Second, Fed credit appears to exhibit greater seasonality whenever interest rates exhibit greater seasonality. Third, when Fed credit does fluctuate seasonally, it reflects seasonality of discount loans and bankers' acceptances but not holdings of government securities. Fourth, the true measure of the opportunity cost of holding reserves in the 1920s is the micro measure which incorporates implicit interest payments to the private banking system. Fifth, the absence of implicit interest payments via the discount window and the centralization of open market operations contributed to the financial panics during the Great Depression. Taken together with the findings on the scissors effect, the evidence presented in this chapter indicates that the relative stability of the 1920s cannot be attributed to fine-tuning by the Fed.

7   The Fed, the executive branch, and public finance, 1934–1939

7.1 Introduction

The decade of the twenties was a period of stability in two senses. As indicated in the last chapter, the decade was one of relative stability in total output produced. Stability in the real economy was accompanied by stability in the government's financing requirements. There were no important shocks which would have led to significant changes in the government's demand for revenue. Accordingly, there were no fundamental changes in monetary institutions during the decade.

The Great Depression upset the stability. The direct effect, of course, was a prolonged period of negative economic growth. The indirect effect was a surge in government financing requirements in its aftermath. This indirect effect is documented in figure 7.1 which shows a measure of permanent government spending (Barro, 1986) over the period 1918–80.[1] The instability in growth and financing led to a flurry of legislative activity representing the most fundamental change in the monetary sector since the founding of the Fed. Legislation was passed which relaxed the gold-backing constraints on the monetary sector, centralized Fed open market operations, established the Treasury as a co-producer of money, introduced upward flexibility in the reserve requirement on retail banks, and created the Federal Deposit Insurance Corporation.

The new monetary environment necessitated a more complex relationship between the government and its monetary agents, which now included the Treasury as well as the Fed. When revenue demands were modest, as in the 1920s, the government could allow a competitively structured Federal Reserve to run more or less on automatic pilot. The best the Fed could do in terms of profits was to "break-even," as was reflected by the fact that little revenue was transferred to the government during most of the decade.

When revenue demands were more substantial (and gold backing less of an issue), as in the 1930s, subtle principle-agent problems arose. For one thing, the government now had to be concerned about how to provide the Treasury with the proper incentives in carrying out its responsibilities as

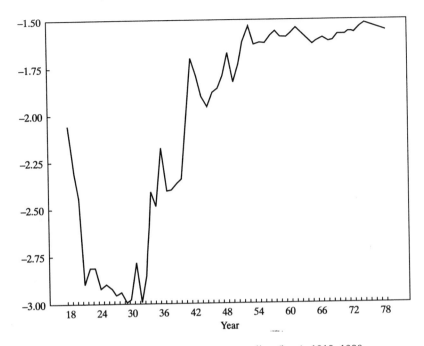

Figure 7.1 Permanent government spending (logs), 1918–1980

co-producer of money. Also, the reserve requirement evolved into an important policy tool in the 1930s and the government had to decide whether decision making rights would be delegated to one of the money producers.

This chapter will focus on the period from 1934 to 1939 and interpret the changes in monetary institutions and monetary policies at this time in the context of the microeconomics model of the reserve industry. The major purpose is to show how the relationship between the Fed and the executive branch was shaped by the government's financing requirements. The secondary purpose is to point out how these spending-induced changes in monetary institutions imposed a severe strain on the financial sector. To some extent, this strain was unavoidable. Financial stability concerns, however, were accommodated within the constraints imposed by the new financing requirements.

7.2 The institutional setting

In the first two years of his administration, Franklin Roosevelt responded to the increased financing requirements associated with the depression by taking actions which increased the seigniorage capacity of the monetary sector and at the same time fundamentally changed the Treasury's monetary authority. A series of executive orders in 1933 established a January 17, 1934 deadline for individuals and banks to deliver their gold coins, bullion and certificates to the Treasury at the official price of $20.67 per ounce. This was followed by congressional enactment of the Gold Reserve Act on January 30, 1934. One feature of this Act required the Fed to surrender its gold holdings to the Treasury in return for gold certificates that did not convey any ownership rights. After 1933, therefore, title to all gold coin and bullion was vested in the Treasury. A second feature formally gave the President discretionary powers to reduce the gold content of the dollar from between 50 to 60 percent of its former content. Because the government was no longer bound by the requirement to keep the dollar price of gold fixed, a significant long-run constraint on the government's monetary powers was relaxed.

This revaluation had important wealth implications for the Treasury. Under the old fixed price system, Treasury wealth did not change when it acquired an ounce of gold by issuing a gold certificate. Any subsequent sale of the ounce had to be at the $20.67 price and it required the retirement of $20.67 of gold certificates (see Friedman and Schwartz, 1963, p. 25). In the post-1933 setting, however, there was some positive probability of future upward revaluation of the official gold price. This implied that any acquisition of gold by the Treasury directly increased its wealth in the sense of creating the opportunity for future profits.

The Treasury did not have to wait long for the first revaluation. On January 31, 1934, the day after the Gold Reserve Act passed, Roosevelt exercised his authority and established a new dollar price of gold at $35 per ounce. In aggregate terms the revaluation generated almost $3 billion in "profits" for the Treasury. The only way the Treasury could realize these profits was by issuing new gold certificates to the Fed and in the process creating new checking balances for itself at the Fed. By spending these balances, the Treasury could increase the monetary base.

With the Gold Reserve Act, the Treasury possessed monetary authority akin to that sometimes enjoyed under the National Bank System. Not only could the Treasury exercise discretion over expenditure of its profits, but the 1934 revaluation also stimulated an inflow of gold which the Treasury could monetize through the issue of new gold certificates to the Fed. These monetary powers were reinforced by the earlier passage of the Thomas Amendment to the Agricultural Adjustment Act in May 1933. One section of the amendment created a silver purchase program that gave the executive branch new powers to issue silver certificates. Another section allowed the President to direct the Secretary of the Treasury to issue US notes or greenbacks up to a total value of $3 billion.

The new gold policy, along with the Thomas amendment, empowered the Treasury to expand the base by considerably more than $10 billion (Crawford, 1972, p. 183). Whether these powers in fact were exercised depended on the President and the Treasury. If the Treasury deemed it appropriate, for instance, it could refuse to issue new gold or silver certificates. The monetary base could even be contracted by withdrawing gold certificates from the Fed or silver certificates from circulation. In terms of the ability to manipulate the monetary base, the Treasury's powers were at least as potent as the Fed's after 1933 (Crawford, 1972, chapter 11).

These institutional changes pertaining to the Treasury's authority to create money coincided with a fundamental change in the legal environment surrounding the Federal Reserve System. Prior to 1933 the Fed was required by the Federal Reserve Act to pay a portion of its net earnings to the Treasury. However, section 4 of the Banking Act of 1933 gave the Fed the right to retain all of its revenue. This financing arrangement was to persist throughout the remainder of the thirties and most of the forties.

Taken together, the change in gold policy and the change in the Fed's financing structure established a unique monetary arrangement. The new monetary constitution gave two agencies money creation powers. After 1933, Federal Reserve System holdings of government securities generated interest earnings which could be spent exclusively on the Fed's operation. The Fed no longer was required to make a transfer payment to the Treasury. Correspondingly, no direct benefits accrued to the Fed through gold inflows into the country. The gold certificate received by the Fed after any inflow did not give it legal title to the gold. In the post-1933 setting, only Treasury wealth increased as a result of the new gold certificates issued.

The Banking Act of 1935 also changed the monetary environment. One section of the Act legally sanctioned the *de facto* centralization of open market operations that had occurred during the Great Depression. Exclusive decision making rights now resided with the Board; individual reserve banks no longer had the right to conduct open market operations for their own accounts. Another section made reserve requirements more flexible. Instead of being fixed by administrative statute, the Act gave the Board limited authority to change the reserve requirement.

A final institutional change was the introduction of federal deposit insurance. The Banking Act of 1933 called upon the Federal Reserve to use $144 million from its surplus account for financing the creation of the Federal Deposit Insurance Corporation. Retail banks which were members of the Fed were required to join the FDIC and all other retail banks had the option. The FDIC would insure deposits up to a limit of $5,000.

Summarizing, there were four institutional changes which changed the monetary environment in the mid 1930s. First, the Banking Act of 1933 and the Gold Reserve Act of 1934 increased the seigniorage capacity of the monetary sector and established the executive branch and the Fed as co-producers of high-powered money with neither having to share money creation revenue with the other. Second, the Banking Act of 1935 centralized open market operations. Third, the 1935 Act also introduced flexibility into reserve requirements. Fourth, the Banking Act of 1933 created federal deposit insurance.

The next section develops the theme that the four institutional changes were adaptations to the government's requirements for more seigniorage. These adaptations led to two monetary problems. One problem stemmed from the duopoly setting. The ability of one government producer (the Treasury) to produce money that was a perfect substitute for the other producer's (the Fed's) money created the type of seigniorage incentive problem discussed by Rolnick, Smith, and Weber (1993, 1994). The other problem was that the relatively high seigniorage requirement interfered with the Fed's ability to service the retail banking sector which tended to expose retail banks to a greater risk of failure.

7.3 Monetary policy

7.3.1 A principle-agent approach

The discussion of the institutional setting as it existed in the 1930s introduces a new decision making variable – reserve requirements on retail banks – that has not to this point played a role in the basic micro model of the Federal Reserve System. The justification for this neglect is that between 1917 and 1935 reserve requirements were fixed by legislative statute. As emphasized above, however, this was no longer true after 1935.

A recent paper of mine (Toma, 1995) has extended the basic micro model to take account of this new factor in a way that emphasizes the principle-agent relationship between the general government and the Federal Reserve. The principle-agent extension is faithful to the basic model in viewing the Federal Reserve as providing clearinghouse services for the retail banking system and for financing general government outlays. The innovative feature is that government, as agent, sets the reserve requirement and then auctions off the right to operate the Fed. The winning bidder is responsible for choosing an implicit interest rate (subsidy rate) on reserves, *given the pre-set reserve requirement*. The implications of this extended model are that movements in subsidies and reserve requirements should be related systematically to changes in the government's revenue needs and to the market rate of interest on bank assets. In particular, when the government requires more revenue from the Fed, it increases the reserve requirement which makes operating the Fed more profitable. The bid payment to the Treasury for operating rights increases and the winning bidder sets a subsidy rate higher than otherwise.

How does the principle-agent "story" match-up with the actual legal setting surrounding Fed money production after the Great Depression? Of course, the government has never literally auctioned operating rights to competing Federal Reserve managers. The auction story does serve, however, as an abstract representation of a more realistic selection process where the head of state says to the Fed appointee: "The administration wants you to serve as the next Fed chair. As you know the revenue needs of the government are acute at this time. Subject to the prevailing reserve requirement, we expect (require) you to turnover $x to be dispersed in annual lump sum payments during your four-year term. The administration respects the Fed's independence. Other than this transfer you are free to conduct the Fed's business as you choose. Do you accept these terms?" The implicit understanding is that if the chair refuses to make the expected transfers, then the President will call upon Congress to change the structure of the Fed in a way that results in immediate dismissal of the chair.

With respect to reserve requirements, the Banking Act of 1933 granted the Fed authority to change requirements during emergencies and the Banking Act of 1935 allowed Fed adjustments in response to general credit conditions. The delegation of authority entailed by the Banking Acts, however, was not unrestricted. Most important, the Act of 1935 proscribed minimum and maximum limits on reserve requirements. Periodically, Congress has adjusted these limits and has debated proposals which, although not ultimately enacted, would have imposed a specific requirement on banks. No such oversight has been evident with respect to Fed subsidy rates. The observation that reserve requirements have typically been at or near their congressionally mandated upper limits, and that Congress has been more involved in overseeing reserve requirements than in subsidy rates, provides a rationale for modeling the government as effectively controlling reserve requirements, even after 1935, while leaving subsidy rates to the discretion of Fed management.[2]

The principle-agent extension of the basic micro model will be used to evaluate two controversial monetary policy issues of the 1934–9 period. First, why was Federal Reserve credit constant from 1934 to 1939? Second, why did reserve requirements on retail banks double from 1936 to 1937?

7.3.2 Constant Federal Reserve credit, 1934–1939

The striking feature of the Fed's monetary policy from 1934 to 1939 was its passivity. Friedman and Schwartz (1963, pp. 512–13) document that "the use of open market operations to influence the volume of Federal Reserve credit outstanding from day to day, week to week, and month to month ceased to be a continuous activity of the System." Despite the constancy of Fed credit, the average annual rate of monetary base growth was 13 percent from 1934 to the end of 1938. All of this growth can be attributed to the monetary capabilities of the Treasury. As indicated earlier, when gold flows into the country the Treasury can create a gold certificate, exchange it for deposits at the Fed, and finally exchange the deposits for gold. While this procedure increases the base, at times the Treasury chose to exercise its discretionary authority by sterilizing the inflows.

The Treasury's emergence as the active monetary authority during this period has proven puzzling. Friedman and Schwartz devote a great deal of space addressing the question: "Why . . . did [the Fed] ask the Treasury on several occasions to take actions that the System could equally well have taken?" (Friedman and Schwartz, 1963, p. 532). They end up explaining away the Treasury's power advantage in a rather ad hoc manner (Friedman and Schwartz, 1963, pp. 532–4).

In providing a more satisfactory answer, the principle-agent extension of the basic model would highlight the importance of the institutional changes brought about by the new seigniorage requirements. In particular, the Banking Acts of 1933 and 1935 and the Gold Reserve Act were important because they (1) created the Treasury as a money producer on par with the Fed, and (2) generated a gold inflow which could be used as the basis of new currency issue. Both (1) and (2) were instrumental in accommodating the government's new seigniorage requirements.

By establishing what was in effect a duopoly in government money production, the new legislation created a monetary dilemma. Each producer was to have a claim to the revenue accruing from its monetary activities. Since one producer, the Treasury, did not have clearinghouse responsibilities, nor did it have any means of making explicit interest payments on its money, this duopoly would be prone to the seigniorage incentive problem outlined by Rolnick, Smith, and Weber (1993, 1994). The source of this problem was that Treasury money was a perfect substitute for Fed money; the Treasury had no way of establishing a demand for its production of monetary base that was separate from the demand for Fed base.

It is in light of the seigniorage incentive problem that monetary policy in the mid 1930s can properly be understood; namely, that the assignment of the active/passive roles by the legislature was an example of the type of policy coordination intended to overcome excessive money production. The Fed policy of constant Federal Reserve credit transformed the Treasury into the monopoly producer of money. Moreover, the assignment of monopoly rights to the Treasury rather than the Fed took advantage of the fact that in the 1930s monetary environment, the Treasury happened to be the low cost producer.

Consider the direct cost of producing money. While Fed money production would not require a large resource expenditure, the open market staff would have to enter the government bond market and negotiate the purchase of a security. The costs of Treasury money production, on the other hand, were as close to zero as economically possible. Given the inflow of gold after the Gold Reserve Act, *and given that the Treasury had to purchase this gold*, the monetary base could be changed at zero resource cost simply by the Treasury adjusting its gold certificate account at the Fed. As long as the general government's seigniorage requirement called for an increase in the monetary base by an amount equal to or less than the total value of gold inflows, the Treasury was the least cost producer of all the additional base.

A second way in which the Treasury enjoyed a cost advantage pertained to the "fiction" of auctioning rights for operating the Fed. According to the auction story, potential Fed managers periodically bid for operating rights with the bid payment going to finance the general government's revenue requirement. Both the auction and the transfer payments would entail reoccurring administrative costs. Alternatively, the Treasury could act as the dominant money producer with the Fed making use of all revenue accruing from its existing portfolio of assets. In this case no auction would have to be conducted and no transfer payment made. Implicitly, Fed officials would be paying the Treasury for operating rights by forgoing their role as the government's money producer. The important point is that in the immediate post-1933 environment production and administrative costs associated with money would be minimized by designating the Treasury as the active party and the Fed as the passive party.[3]

7.3.3 The 1936–1937 reserve requirement increases

One of the most controversial monetary policies in the Fed's history was the doubling of reserve requirements on retail banks from 1936 to 1937. A traditional textbook account of how reserve requirements are set would tend to emphasize a stabilization objective. The government lowers reserve requirements when real economic activity is below its long-run trend and raises the requirement when it is above trend.

The difficulty with the textbook explanation as applied to the 1936–7 case is illustrated in figure 7.2. Using traditional decomposition methods, the detrended real GNP is plotted against the change in the (log of the) reserve requirement. The 1936–7 doubling of requirements occurred during a period when economic activity was significantly below trend. Clearly, this policy cannot be defended on stabilization grounds. Indeed, the traditional

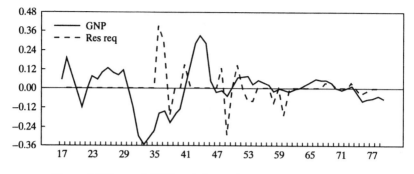

Figure 7.2 Detrend GNP and change in reserve requirement (logs)

interpretation is that it represented a misguided attempt by the Fed in the midst of a depressed economy to reduce the excess reserves held by the banking system (Barro, 1993, p. 482).

According to the principle-agent approach, the primary driving force behind a reserve requirement increase would be an increase in the government's financing needs. Figure 7.3 superimposes a plot (in levels and differences) of the log of the reserve requirement on permanent government spending from figure 7.1. The principle-agent approach would attribute the absence of variation in the reserve requirement from 1917 to the mid 1930s to the low volatility (post-World War I) of permanent government spending. Once it became evident that permanent government spending was increasing in the aftermath of the Great Depression, and in general had become more volatile, Congress reacted by passing the Banking Acts of 1933 and 1935 which changed the mechanism for setting reserve requirements in a way that would be expected to generate more flexibility. In the near term, the government's financing objective and the Fed's earning objective called for the same policy – an increase in the reserve requirement. This is precisely what occurred with the doubling of reserve requirements in 1936 and 1937 to their new statutory upper limits.[4]

7.4 Conclusion

Monetary theorists have criticized the reserve requirement increases in the 1930s for depressing real output. While a strong case can be made that reserve requirements delayed the recovery from the Great Depression, this chapter has argued that the standard critique misses the mark. Policies must be judged against viable alternatives. If reserve requirements had not been increased, then seigniorage revenue would have been lower and the government would have been forced to turn to non-seigniorage sources to finance

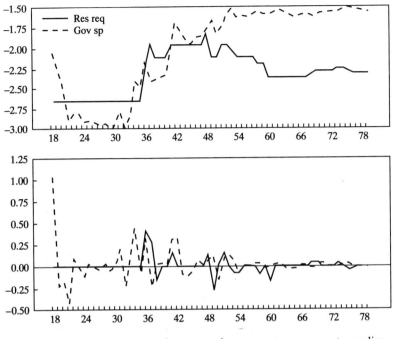

Figure 7.3 Reserve requirement and permanent government spending (logs)

the government's revenue requirements. Current and prospective income tax rates would have been higher which would have had its own depressing effects on the economy.

The policy chosen – increases in reserve requirements and increases in tax rates – was optimal in that it spread the cost of satisfying the revenue requirement among different groups.[5] The higher reserve requirements increased costs to the financial system and the higher tax rates increased costs to income earners. Policy makers, of course, were aware of these increased costs. Passage of federal deposit insurance was one way they hoped to moderate the adverse stability implications for the financial system.

8 World War II financing

8.1 Introduction

Several changes in the early 1940s economic environment affected the relationship between the public, the Fed, and the Treasury. Most important, government financing requirements increased throughout most of the decade (see figure 7.1). Also, after 1940 the rate of gold inflow into the United States slowed markedly. This created a situation where the government's desired rate of money production generally exceeded the amount that the Treasury could produce on the basis of its gold purchases. The 1930s arrangement giving the Treasury sole rights to produce new money no longer was satisfactory. The task now facing the general government was how to supplement the Treasury's money production without reintroducing the seigniorage incentive problem emphasized in the previous chapter.

The solution took the form of an interest rate control program. In April 1942 the United States Treasury and the Federal Reserve agreed to control nominal interest rates on short-term and long-term government securities. With respect to short-term securities, the Fed announced that it would buy at a rate of 3/8 percent all 3-month Treasury bills presented by the public. Later, in August 1942 the Fed also announced that the original seller of a Treasury bill would be able to repurchase the bill at the 3/8 percent rate. As a result, the rate on 3-month Treasury bills was constant from 1943 to the end of the bill rate policy in July 1947.

The agreement on longer-term securities did not take the form of a rigid promise to buy and resell securities at fixed rates. Of particular interest, the Fed agreed to support 25-year government bond prices at a level consistent with a 2.5 percent interest rate ceiling. While the Treasury and Fed ended the bill rate peg by mutual consent in July 1947, the ceiling on 25-year government bond rates lasted until the Accord of March 1951.

Traditionally, economists have viewed the 1940s interest rate control program as an attempt to peg all government security rates at levels that were too low to be sustained. According to this view, the Fed may be able to temporarily lower the market interest rate by expanding the money supply to reduce the real interest rate. Over the longer run, however, the real rate returns toward its natural level and the Fed must expand the money supply at a faster rate. Under these circumstances, the program eventually must be abandoned because it leads to excessive debt monetization and an inflation explosion.

Recent theoretical work offers a different perspective for assessing the general issue of interest rate pegs. The new view is based on a monetary environment where gold convertibility constraints do not preclude some flexibility in long-run monetary policy. The new view also assumes that the policy maker knows he cannot manipulate the real interest rate and that the public uses rational expectations in forming their forecasts of future inflation. By committing to a particular money supply process, the policy maker can control inflation expectations and thereby control the market interest rate.

According to the new view, a sustainable policy that pegs the market rate at a low level has two desirable features. First, it protects against over issue by committing the policy maker to moderate long-run money growth rates. Second, it elevates current and prospective demands for money by constraining the public's inflation expectations. As a result, the government is able to raise significant amounts of seigniorage.

Somewhat surprisingly, there has been little attempt to apply the new view to the 1940s when policy makers in the United States explicitly committed to interest rate controls. One possible reason for this lack of interest is that a cursory examination of the 1940s evidence seems at odds with the general prediction of the new view that the public expected monetary restraint on average. Money growth rates from 1942–4 equaled about 20 percent per year. Given this wartime monetary expansion, it seems implausible that a market rate on long-term bonds, reflecting rational expectations of long-term inflation, would have been low.

There are a few studies, however, which do take seriously the possibility that the new view, properly reformulated, can explain how the low rates on long-term government bonds were sustained throughout the 1940s. For instance, I (Toma, 1985; 1991b) have focused on the wartime period and have argued that the 2.5 percent long-term interest rate ceiling allowed for monetary expansion in the near-term (1942–4) as long as the public expected monetary restraint later. Eichengreen and Garber (1991) have focused on the postwar period and have argued that the Federal Reserve could implement the interest rate ceiling policy by committing to an implicit target zone for the price level. From 1945 to 1950 the Federal Reserve responded to exogenous increases in real interest rates, that drove the price level to the upper range of the zone, by reducing the money supply. As a result of unexpected events, however, policy makers in the early 1950s were soon unwilling to reduce the money supply to required levels and the ceiling commitment on long-term government bonds was abandoned in March 1951.

As outlined in the next section, Eichengreen and Garber's explanation implies that the government adopted the interest rate program for financial stability reasons. In contrast, my work is based on a seigniorage motive. The theme of this chapter is that seigniorage was the driving force with financial stability entering as an important secondary consideration. In developing this theme it will be important to point out that the way the government controlled short-term interest rates in the 1940s was fundamentally different from the way it controlled long-term rates. Unlike the long-term rate, the short-term rate was an administered rate that was set below market.

8.2 The policy environment of the 1940s

The 1942 Fed and Treasury interest rate control agreement applied to the whole spectrum of government security rates. At the short end, the Fed agreed to freely buy and resell 3-month Treasury bills at a rate of 3/8 percent. For other government securities, the Fed and Treasury committed only to a policy of taking actions to prevent their yields from rising above a certain level – ranging from roughly 0.875 percent for certificates to 0.9 percent for 13-month notes, 1.5 percent for four-and-a-half-year notes, and 2.5 percent for 25-year bonds. To simplify the analysis, I shall focus on the 3/8 percent bill rate peg and the 2.5 percent ceiling on long-term government bond rates.

The rational expectations perspective suggests that the Fed and Treasury agreed to control interest rates as a means of avoiding the seigniorage incentive problem; that is, as a means of avoiding persistently high money growth rates and inflation. But why should the government be more concerned with persistent inflation in the 1940s than in previous periods? One explanation (see Toma, 1985) emphasizes the unique monetary environment of the 1940s where (1) there were dual producers of government money, (2) money and debt creation were to be relied upon as sources of revenue for financing the increased military requirement associated with the war, and (3) there was no mechanism (such as a gold standard) to anchor the public's long-run inflation expectations. Under these circumstances, the amount of real seigniorage that the government could raise would depend on public confidence that the real value of money and debt would not be inflated away after the war.

A related explanation emphasizes the government's desire to avoid financial instability. Recalling a thesis advanced by economic analysts in the 1940s, Eichengreen and Garber argue that "the banking system had grown increasingly vulnerable to declining bond prices as a result of its massive investments in government securities over the course of World War II" (1991, p. 197) . A corollary of the financial instability thesis is that the very act of committing to the 2.5 percent ceiling tended to insure its durability.

the decision in favor of the 2.5 percent rate taken at the time of Pearl Harbor made any future change in the rate extremely difficult – as it resulted, on the one hand, in building up a tremendous volume of assets on the books of financial institutions which are worth par only on a 2.5 percent basis and, on the other hand, in building up a large volume of liabilities of these institutions which can be serviced only if 2.5 percent can be obtained on the corresponding assets.   (Murphy, 1950, p. 94)

Both the seigniorage and financial stability explanations point to the promise of long-run monetary restraint, as embodied in the long-term interest rate ceiling, as the central feature of the 1940s program. This is consistent with the Fed and Treasury's own understanding of the program. Federal Reserve officials repeatedly issued policy statements to assure the public that their primary concern was to maintain the credit of the United States by preserving the purchasing power of the dollar. Fed officials also expressed concern for the stability of the financial system. The Board of Governors warned that

A major consequence . . . of . . . increasing the general level of interest rates would be a fall in the market values of outstanding Government securities. These price declines would create difficult market problems for the Treasury in refunding its maturing and called securities. If the price declines were sharp they could have highly unfavorable repercussions on the functioning of financial institutions and if carried far enough might even weaken public confidence in such institutions.
(Board of Governors, 1945, p. 7)

Interestingly, there was little controversy over whether 2.5 percent was the appropriate ceiling for the long-term interest rate. Using the recent past as a guide, the Fed and Treasury tended to view 2.5 percent as "the rate which had been established by the 'natural' forces of the market" (Murphy, 1950, p. 93).

In contrast, the 3/8 percent bill rate policy was controversial. Prevailing bill rates at the end of 1941 and the beginning of 1942 equaled about 1/4 percent. The Fed preferred that the bill rate, like the long-term rate, be set and maintained as a market rate. The Fed insisted that it would be able to achieve any bill rate target simply by announcing its intention to do so and then conducting monetary policy in the ordinary way through discretionary open market operations. The Treasury, on the other hand, was skeptical that the Fed would be able to control market rates on short-term and long-term bonds simultaneously.

The dispute ended on April 30, 1942 with the establishment of a "posted" bill rate that represented a rejection of the ordinary way of conducting open market operations.

The decision to 'post' a buying rate for Treasury bills (rather than to purchase them by individual negotiation) followed the precedent which had been set long before in the case of Federal Reserve purchases of bankers' acceptances but had never previously been applied to government securities. There was considerable discussion of the level at which the rate should be posted. Treasury officials proposed 1/4 percent but agreed to the Federal Reserve counterproposal of 3/8 percent.

(Murphy, 1950, p. 98)

The posting policy was analogous to a discount policy. Any slight change in market conditions, which resulted in the 3/8 percent peg being below market, would force the Fed into a position of acquiring outstanding bills. Unlike the long-term interest rate ceiling, which was expected to last at least through the war and postwar transition, the 3/8 percent bill rate peg was perceived as a short-run method of supplying reserves to banks.

8.3 The theory of interest rate pegs

There are two types of interest rate pegs to be considered: one in which only the long-term government bond rate is pegged, and a dual peg that tries to control both the long-term government bond rate and the short-term bill rate. With respect to the single peg, economists have used the rational-expectations assumption to evaluate a policy of pegging a one-period interest rate with a money supply rule (see Cover and Schutte, 1990); but the analysis can be generalized to a peg on an n-period rate. Under simplifying assumptions, the nominal rate $(r_{n,t})$ on an n-period government bond is the same as the nominal rate $(i_{n,t})$ on an n-period private bond in period t:

$$r_{n,t}=i_{n,t}=c+(u_t+E_tp_{t+n}-p_t)/n, \tag{8.1}$$

where the real rate of interest on a one-period bond in period t equals a time-invariant permanent component c plus a random disturbance term u_t with a fixed mean of zero and finite variance, E_tp_{t+n} is the mathematical expectation of p_{t+n} conditioned on information available in period t, and p_t is the log of the general price level.[1]

Finally, assume a standard demand function for real money balances in period t such that

$$m_t-p_t=a_0-a_1r_{1,t}+a_2y_t+v_t \tag{8.2}$$

where m_t and y_t are the logs of the money supply and real income; a_0, a_1, and a_2 are constants; and v_t is randomly distributed with a fixed mean of zero and finite variance.

Equations (8.1) and (8.2) can be used to derive a condition for pegging the n-period market interest rate. A peg of particular interest, given the 1940s policy environment, is one where the policy maker fixes the market rate at the permanent real rate, c. For all $j > 0$, a commitment of this type results in the condition:

$$E_t r_{n,t+j} = c \text{ if and only if } E_t(m_{t+1} - m_t)^* = a_2 E_t(y_{t+1} - y_t) - (u_t + v_t) \quad (8.3)$$

where * indicates the pegging solution (the derivation is presented in the appendix). According to (8.3), a pegging policy requires that the expected money supply growth rate from t to $t+1$ differs from the weighted expected real income growth rate when the sum of the current disturbances are non-zero. With a negative shock ($u_t < 0$) to the real interest rate, for instance, the policy maker must commit to a money growth rate that exceeds the weighted real income growth rate. Because the public in t would expect that the real interest rate would return to c in the next period (that is, $E_t u_{t+1} = 0$), they would also expect the money growth rate from $t+1$ to $t+2$ to return to its normal level. This pattern of monetary expansion followed by restraint is relevant for the 1940s because controls on the production process during the war may have temporarily decreased short-term interest rates (see Friedman and Schwartz, 1963; Rockoff, 1984; Toma, 1991b).

Under a dual interest rate program, the central bank would announce a money supply rule that satisfied the condition in equation (8.3) for a long-term bond ($n > 1$). At the same time, the government would attempt to control short-term interest rates. In particular, consider a policy (which I later show to be relevant for the 1940s) in which the Treasury would post an interest rate p on one-period government bonds for the upcoming period such that p is less than the expected market rate c on a one-period bond, and the central bank would announce its willingness to buy and resell those short-term bonds at the posted rate. With $p < c = E_t i_{1,t+1}$, individuals would expect to hold 1-period private bonds rather than 1-period government bonds in $t+1$. All new one-period bonds issued by the Treasury would be bought by the central bank, perhaps simply to replace the maturing 1-period securities in its portfolio. In this special case, pegging the one-period government bond rate would not directly result in any money supply change. More generally, the amount of new one-period government bonds issued by the Treasury in $t+1$ would be less or greater than the central bank's holdings of 1-period government bonds in t.

If we assume the central bank did not conduct offsetting open-market sales of longer-term securities – perhaps because its portfolio contained no longer-term bonds – then the debt monetization process inherent in the short-term interest rate peg would establish a minimum expected money growth rate from t to $t+1$. If this minimum rate equaled the equation (8.3) solution, $E(m_{t+1}-m_t)^*$, then monetization of 1-period bonds would automatically generate a money supply growth rate consistent with the long-term interest rate peg. A minimum growth rate less than $E(m_{t+1}-m_t)^*$ would present no problem; the central bank could maintain the long-term interest rate peg by supplementing the automatic debt monetization of one-period bonds with the right amount of open market purchases of long-term bonds. Should the minimum money supply growth rate exceed $E(m_{t+1}-m_t)^*$, however, the policy of standing ready to buy 1-period government bonds at a below-market rate would raise inflation expectations to a level that would not sustain the long-term peg.

8.4 Competing hypotheses and the evidence

The conventional and the long-run monetary restraint views of the 1940s program can be interpreted as special cases of the theory of a dual interest rate program. According to the conventional view, the program was not sustainable because the public expected the Treasury to pursue a policy of financing the war by relying heavily, perhaps exclusively, on short-term debt issues that would be monetized by the Federal Reserve under the passive pegging policy. In contrast, the long-run monetary restraint view is that the Treasury and Fed were implicitly committed to future money growth rates that would be consistent with low long-run inflation and at the same time would restrict the quantity of government bonds that would be covered by the 3/8 percent peg.

Although there is no definitive way of ascertaining the public's expectations about the scope of the bill rate policy, it seems reasonable that the public did not expect that all future debt outside the Treasury would be short term. For one thing, the bill rate policy had much in common with the Fed's discount policy during World War I in that the discount rate was set below the market rate and loans to member banks required federal securities as collateral. From June 1917 to June 1920, discounts increased by about 2.5 billion dollars, while total debt outside the Treasury increased by over 20 billion dollars. To the extent the public used the World War I experience as a guide, they would not have anticipated that bills issued by the Treasury, and acquired by the Fed, would comprise a large share of the total debt outside the Treasury. Also, the direct connection between bills issued and bills monetized during World War II was widely understood at the time which must have helped reduce the likelihood of excessive issues. In fact, the Fed encouraged limits on the weekly issues of new Treasury bills throughout the pegging period, although Treasury pressure sometimes served as a countervailing force.

The evidence in table 8.1 confirms that the public in March 1942 would

Table 8.1 *US government securities outside the Treasury and the monetary base, 1942–1950 (in $ billions)*

| (1) | Securities outside the Treasury | | | |
	All securities (2)	Bills (3)	Coupon issues with maturity of less than one year (4)	Monetary base (5)
March 1942	48.9	1.7	2.2	24.5
March 1943	83.8	9.2	15.8	29.1
March 1944	129.6	13.1	33.5	33.2
March 1945	163.4	16.9	43.0	40.5
March 1946	197.1	17.0	52.5	43.7
March 1947	172.5	17.0	36.1	44.3
March 1948	161.4	13.9	35.9	44.9
March 1949	155.7	11.6	37.6	46.9
March 1950	154.5	12.3	36.9	43.0

Sources: Board of Governors, *Banking and Monetary Statistics* (1976), table 13.5, p. 884 for columns (2)–(4) and Friedman and Schwartz, *Monetary History of the United States* (1963), table B-3, pp. 805–6 for column (5).

have been mistaken in expecting that all future debt outside the Treasury would be short term. Throughout the 1940s most of the outstanding debt was due to mature in more than one year. By March 1946, total bills outstanding equaled 17 billion dollars, less than one-year coupon issues equaled 52.5 billion dollars, and longer-term debt equaled 127.6 billion dollars. Also, Toma (1992) documents that by the end of 1946 the Fed had acquired (monetized) over 90 percent of outstanding bills.

Although it is unlikely that the public in March 1942 perfectly foresaw the actual post-1942 division of total debt between bills, less than 1-year coupon issues, and longer-term securities as depicted in table 8.1, there is no reason to suspect that they systematically would have underestimated or overestimated the proportion of short-term to long-term securities outstanding. For estimation purposes, therefore, I assume that the actual post-1942 division represented the public's optimal prediction and that it was generally understood that the Fed eventually would acquire the bills. If the public had expected only 3-month bills would be monetized, then the minimum annualized rate of base growth from March 1942 to March 1946 would have been about 13 percent.[2]

Is the 13 percent figure consistent with the pegging condition shown in

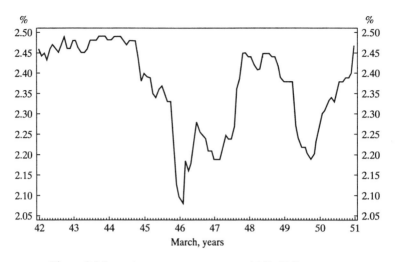

Figure 8.1 Long-term government rates, 1942–1951

equation (8.3)? Substituting upper and lower estimates for the other parameter values into (8.3) provides limits on the wartime money supply growth rate necessary to peg the market rate on an n-period bond at a value of c in the current and all future periods:

$$E_t r_{n,t+j} = c \text{ if and only if } 0.04 \leq E_t(m_{t+1} - m_t)^* \leq 0.22. \tag{8.4}$$

Therefore, a peg narrowly covering 3-month bills would generate a wartime money supply growth rate (13 percent) roughly consistent with condition (8.4).[3] Based on this evidence regarding the short-term peg, the dual interest rate program was sustainable.

A narrowly defined short-term rate peg was only one component of a sustainable dual interest rate program. The other component entailed a commitment of long-run monetary restraint that kept market interest rates on 25-year government bonds at or below 2.5 percent. Therefore, a prerequisite for the long-run monetary restraint view is that the 25-year government bond rate be a market-determined rate.

Figure 8.1 shows the long-term government rate and figure 8.2 shows the spread between a private long-term interest rate, Moody's Aaa corporate rate, and the long-term government rate from 1942 to 1951. Even though the long-term government rate was relatively constant during World War II, there was no tendency for the rate spread to increase as would be the case if the long-term rate was an administered below market rate.[4] In fact, the rate spread fell throughout much of 1942 and 1943 and then fluctuated around a value of about 0.25 for the rest of the war. After the war, the rate

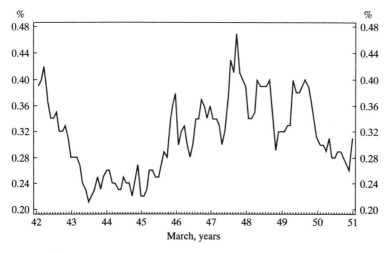

Figure 8.2 Long-term spread, 1942–1951

spread varied from a low of about 0.25 to a high of about 0.50. The average level and variability of the rate spread throughout the 1940s is in line with the experience in the years preceding and following the interest rate program.

Finally, table 8.2 shows long-term government bonds (coupon issues over ten years) held by the Fed and the private sector as a fraction of the total amount outside the Treasury. The data indicate that the public had no special incentive to abandon long-term government bonds at any stage of the war. Throughout the war, private sector holdings of long-term government bonds equaled about 90 percent and Fed holdings equaled 3 percent or less of the total outside the Treasury. The private sector percentage fell somewhat in 1948, reflecting Fed purchases of long-term bonds, but then stabilized around 80 percent for the rest of the decade. The evidence indicates that, unlike Treasury bills, long-term government bonds were not governed by an endogenous debt monetization process. Indeed, the public's willingness to hold these securities, given the privately issued alternatives, suggests that the public's long-run inflation expectations in the 1940s must have been relatively low: no higher than the difference between 2.5 percent and the sum of the term premium and the long-term real interest rate.

8.5 *Ex post* monetary growth rates and the 1951 Accord

According to the long-run monetary restraint view, a negative shock to the short-term real interest rate during the war would allow the money growth

Table 8.2 *Ownership of US government securities with maturity greater than ten years, 1942–1950*

Date (1)	Total outstanding (in $ billions) (2)	Fraction of total	
		Fed (3)	Private (4)
1942 June	12.5	0.03	0.89
Dec.	16.6	0.03	0.89
1943 June	19.6	0.01	0.90
Dec.	23.4	0.01	0.90
1944 June	31.3	0.01	0.89
Dec.	35.1	0.01	0.89
1945 June	44.4	0.005	0.90
Dec.	59.8	0.002	0.91
1946 June	59.6	0.002	0.90
Dec.	54.8	0.002	0.91
1947 June	54.8	0.002	0.92
Dec.	54.8	0.002	0.91
1948 June	53.9	0.05	0.86
Dec.	53.9	0.13	0.78
1949 June	48.6	0.09	0.82
Dec.	45.1	0.08	0.82
1950 June	45.1	0.05	0.85
Dec.	43.6	0.06	0.83

Note:
The table does not show ownership by (non-Fed) US government agencies and trust funds.
Source: Board of Governors, *Banking and Monetary Statistics* (1976), table 13.5, p. 884.

rate to exceed the weighted real income growth rate. Once wartime controls ended, short-term real rates would rise to normal levels and the government's commitment to the long-term interest rate ceiling would require postwar monetary restraint. The dual interest rate program was sustainable, therefore, only if the public expected wartime monetary expansion to be followed by relatively low rates of money growth. One factor that would have reinforced this expectation was the monetary record from the recent past. As Friedman and Schwartz point out, a post World War II expectation of monetary restraint was "partly a product of the severe 1929–33 contraction,

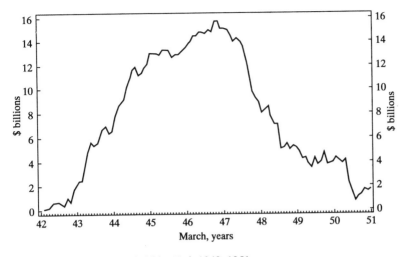

Figure 8.3 Bills held by Fed, 1942–1951

which fostered a belief that severe contractions were the peacetime danger if not indeed the norm; and partly a product of the 1920–1 price collapse, which fostered a belief that major wars were followed by deflation and depression" (Friedman and Schwartz, 1963, p. 585).

Federal Reserve policy during the 1940s was consistent with the expectation of postwar monetary restraint (see table 8.1, column 5). First, note that the change in the monetary base of about 20 billion dollars over the life of the bill rate policy (1942–7) turned out to be only somewhat higher than the 17 billion dollar change that would have resulted if all bills had been monetized. The actual change, in other words, is roughly in line with the change the public might rationally have expected from a below market short-term rate pegging policy with narrow coverage, supplemented by small amounts of Fed-initiated purchases of longer-term debt. Figure 8.3 shows that after July 1947 the endogenous debt monetization process reversed itself and by the end of 1950 Fed bill holdings were near zero. The base rate of growth from 1947 to 1950 was close to zero as the Fed replaced bills with longer-term bonds.

Even though government officials in the 1940s repeatedly assured the public of their commitment to long-run monetary restraint, the government defaulted on this commitment in March 1951 with the Fed and Treasury Accord. Monetary expansion in the 1950s and 1960s turned out to be inconsistent with the 1940s ceiling of 2.5 percent on the long-term government bond rate. Grossman (1990) attributes violation of the ceiling commitment to surprise increases in the government's revenue requirement after the war that called for increases in revenue from a number of sources, including money creation. He concludes that "the competing claims on national resources that materialized after World War II – especially the costs of postwar reconstruction, the welfare state, and the cold War – were unforeseeable but verifiable contingencies that made partial default excusable" (Grossman, 1990, p. 180).

The unexpected increase in the government's revenue requirement after the war also helps explain a peculiar aspect of the Fed's financing structure during the war and a change in the Fed's financing structure in July 1947. Prior to 1947, the Fed contributed to wartime financing by buying Treasury bills at below market rates. What was peculiar is that the Fed did not make direct transfers to the government, but instead used excess open market operation revenue to build up its surplus account. By 1947, the surplus reached 140 billion dollars. Why did the Fed allow such a buildup? Why not transfer the excess to the Treasury on a regular basis or pass the excess along to the banking system in the form of higher explicit or implicit interest payments?

One interpretation that is consistent with a government financing view is that during the war there was a significant degree of uncertainty about the length of the war and the time path of government spending after the war. If the expectation had been that the war would be a short one and that wartime spending would be followed by substantially lower peacetime spending then excess wartime revenue would have been passed along to the banking system in the form of explicit or implicit interest payments. Alternatively, if it had been known that the war would be a long one followed by substantially higher peacetime spending then excess wartime revenue would have been transferred to the government. Given uncertainty, the optimal strategy was for the Fed to reject both payment methods and instead accumulate an "insurance fund."

By 1947 it was clear that the second scenario was the relevant one: significant government revenue demands would persist into the future. The response was twofold. First, the bill rate policy, which from the beginning was perceived to be temporary, was allowed to lapse. Second, the Fed transferred funds out of its surplus account into the Treasury's account and instituted a policy of transferring excess funds to the Treasury on an annual basis. These transfers have continued up to the present time. Currently, over 90 percent of Fed revenue is transferred to the Treasury.

8.6 Conclusion

The interest rate control program was enacted in the context of a wartime environment that placed looser gold constraints on monetary policy than those which had existed in the early days of the Fed. In the absence of some type of policy coordination between the two money producers of the time – the Fed and Treasury – monetary policy would have been subject to a seigniorage incentive problem. Coordination in the form of the interest rate control program can be interpreted as a substitute for a more formal gold standard regime.

In explaining how the program substituted for a gold standard, this chapter took into account the dual nature of the program. The program involved a commitment on short-term and long-term government bond rates. The Federal Reserve's bill rate policy from 1942–7 was more like a modern-day discount rate policy than an open market operation policy. The Federal Reserve passively accepted 3-month Treasury bills at a rate that was below the market rate on coupon issues with three months to maturity. Because of this artificially low bill rate, bills were driven out of the market and into the portfolio of the Federal Reserve over this period.

Given the debt monetization process associated with the short-term rate peg, why did the interest rate control program result in so little inflation in the 1940s? The answer lies in the scope of coverage of the pegging policy. If the pegging policy had applied to all short-term securities, or even more dramatically to all government securities, then the 1940s interest rate program would have raised inflation expectations and become an engine of inflation as predicted by the conventional view. Because the Federal Reserve's "discount window" (that is, the policy of freely buying securities at a low rate) serviced only 3-month Treasury bills, it was not inherently inflationary.

The overall conclusion of this chapter is that the interest rate control program was first and foremost a financing device. It was no accident, however, that the program had desirable financial stability properties. In fact, there was a conscious attempt to design the program so that financial stability concerns would help insure its credibility. Moreover, this chapter has argued that the program ultimately was abandoned for revenue reasons and not for stability or inflationary concerns. The financing demands accompanying the Korean war represented the last straw – it "made partial default excusable."

Appendix Derivation of equation (8.3)

To derive equation (8.3) in the text, consider that equation (8.2) implies that the price level at t varies with m_t, y_t, u_t, v_t, and with $E_t p_{t+1}$ and also that $E_t p_{t+1}$ depends on $E_t m_{t+1}$, $E_t y_{t+1}$, and $E_t p_{t+2}$, and so on. Through repeated substitution, the current price level and all expected future price levels can be eliminated from equation (8.1). This gives

$$r_{n,t}=c+\{u_t+v_t+\Sigma\ [a_1/(1+a_1)]^j$$
$$E_t[(m_{t+n+j}-m_{t+j})-a_2(y_{t+n+j}-y_{t+j})]\}/n(1+a_1). \tag{A8.1}$$

Substituting c for $r_{n,t}$ in equation (A8.1) gives a condition for pegging the n-period market interest rate in period t at the permanent real rate

$$r_{n,t}=c \text{ iff } \Sigma\ [a_1/(1+a_1)]^j\ E_t[(m_{t+n+j}-m_{t+j})-a_2(y_{t+n+j}-y_{t+j})]=-u_t-v_t.$$
$$\tag{A8.2}$$

To provide more structure to the pegging condition, assume that in planning the money supply growth rate for periods t to $t+1$ the policy maker cannot credibly commit to money growth rates for subsequent periods ($t+1$ to $t+2$, $t+2$ to $t+3$, . . .) that are expected to result in deflation. Since $E_t u_{t+j}=0$, for all $j>0$, equation (8.1) in the text indicates that a commitment to price stability after $t+1$ is equivalent to a commitment to peg the n-period bond rate at c for $t+1$ and beyond. This commitment requires that the expected 1-period rate of growth in the money supply in any future period equals the weighted expected 1-period rate of growth in real income in that period; that is, $E_t[(m_{t+1+j}-m_{t+j})-a_2(y_{t+1+j}-y_{t+j})]=0$, for all $j>0$. Making this substitution into equation (A8.2) gives pegging condition (8.3) in the text.

9 Historical lessons

9.1 Monetary unions

The historical approach to monetary economics is valuable to the extent that it informs the study of monetary events in other time periods. In this sense the historical approach to the Fed has much to offer the modern monetary economist. Consider, for instance, the renewed interest in monetary unions as a way of coordinating policy among a pre-existing group of monetary authorities. A monetary union may be formed by (1) replacing the moneys of the authorities with a single money or (2) retaining the identity of the moneys but fixing the rate at which any one money exchanges with another. While it is natural to think of a single body directing monetary policy in the first setting, the question arises in the second setting whether decision making will be centralized or decentralized. Moreover, how does the nature of the monetary equilibrium depend on centralization versus decentralization?

The Federal Reserve System can be used as the standard of reference in evaluating the performance of a monetary union of the second type. As reviewed in earlier chapters, Rolnick and Weber (1989) have most forcefully stated the case for viewing the 12 Federal Reserve banks as comprising a monetary union: each of the 12 Federal Reserve banks issues a distinct currency which can be traded for the other Federal Reserve currencies at a fixed rate of exchange (at par). According to Rolnick and Weber, if the reserve banks operated independently, then they would be prone to over issue money. The modern Fed has been able to overcome this problem only because monetary decisions have been centralized instead of being left to the discretion of the individual reserve banks.

One issue overlooked by Rolnick and Weber is that Fed policy has not always been centralized. What of the period before the 1930s when reserve banks conducted monetary policy on their own behalf and importantly claimed the seigniorage from their policy? Was monetary policy in this early period in some sense defective because of the lack of coordination? Was it plagued by free-rider problems?

A recent paper by Barry Eichengreen (1992) critiques this early Fed period with the intent of providing a lesson for the founders of the European Monetary Union. The title and subtitle of the paper are revealing: "How Ben Strong would have done it. *European Monetary Union: Lessons and Pitfalls from the Early Fed.*" In keeping with the Rolnick and Weber theme, Eichengreen argues that the history of the early Federal Reserve System provides a guide for how *not* to structure a unified monetary system.

Eichengreen starts out his lesson by drawing the analogy between the early Fed System and the transition to European Monetary Union.

US monetary policy makers would regard it as bizarre, inefficient and dangerous to delegate monetary policy decisions to individual reserve banks. Yet this is precisely what Europe proposes to do during Stage II of the transition to monetary union.

Ironically, the US made this very same mistake following the establishment of the Federal Reserve System. In its early years, the individual reserve banks, while issuing bank notes that traded at fixed exchange rates *vis-à-vis* one another, essentially controlled their own monetary policies. Only as American officials came to appreciate the problems posed by this arrangement was control over policy transferred to Washington DC. The broad outline of policy came to be determined by the Federal Reserve Board and by an Open Market Committee on which Board members and a rotating subset of reserve bank officials sat. But implementation, especially of open market purchases, remained a matter for the individual reserve banks. As late as the 1930s, district reserve banks could still opt out of System transactions. Only after authority was definitely centralized in the hands of the Board of Governors and the Open Market Committee by the Banking Acts of 1933 and 1935 did the new institution begin to operate smoothly.   (1992, pp. 36–7)

Elsewhere in the article, Eichengreen reiterates his main point: "free-rider problems are avoided by the centralization of authority" (1992, p. 36).

Eichengreen uses four vignettes to illustrate the problems associated with decentralization. From my perspective, what is interesting about these examples is that they are taken from the late twenties and early thirties (1927, October 1929, 1932, and March 1933) when policy was becoming increasingly centralized. Rather than indicating the problems with decentralization, they really illustrate the difficulties an industry faces when it tries to hold together an effective cartel in the absence of legally enforced sanctions.

Consider each of Eichengreen's policy failures. The first occurred in the midst of the 1927 recession. Policy failed in this case because the System's cartel body – the Board – had trouble reaching a consensus on a discount rate decrease. The second policy failure occurred during the stock market crash in October 1929. Eichengreen chastises the Fed for failing to pursue a vigorous open market operation policy in the aftermath of the crash. But the failure to respond in a timely manner cannot be blamed on independent open market operations, or the lack thereof. By 1929, open market operations had become increasingly centralized within the Open Market Investment Committee. My rejoinder to Eichengreen would be that policy failed in 1929, just as it did in 1927, because of the increased centralization. Indeed, Harrison, who was the head of the New York Fed, wanted his bank to increase government security purchases and wanted others to be granted the freedom to do likewise. But as even Eichengreen himself points out, Harrison "was called on the carpet" by the Board for his advocacy of independent open market operations and the System, for its part, was unable to "engineer a concerted response to the slump" (Eichengreen, 1992, p. 37).

Eichengreen's policy failures in 1932 and 1933 followed a similar storyline. They are examples of the problems which can arise when a cartel body attempts to enforce a cartel solution in the absence of a foolproof enforcement mechanism. Simply stated, they occurred in my view (see chapter 6) because the Board shut down the discount window and individual reserve banks were not allowed to fill the void by conducting independent open market operations.

The microeconomics model developed in this book argues that a truly decentralized monetary union need not produce the negative consequences alluded to by Eichengreen. *Given the appropriate microfoundations*, competition in the market for central bank money will produce equilibrium outcomes analogous to the outcomes one typically observes in more standard market settings. The most important precondition is that money producers be capable of competing along some dimension that allows them to direct the benefits associated with their output towards those customers who "buy" that output. Accordingly, competition will increase implicit or explicit interest, reduce profits, reduce holding costs, and increase the amount of aggregate real money holdings.

It is the early and mid 1920s, rather than the late 1920s and early 1930s, that represents the best test period for the competitive model. The lessons of the 1920s were not ones concerning the power and effectiveness of a monetary cartel, but ones of the power and effectiveness of the market. The microeconomics approach would point out that the relatively modest government revenue and gold backing requirements of the 1920s allowed the government to chose, or at least tolerate, a highly competitive structure for the Federal Reserve System. Competition among reserve banks in conducting open market operations, particularly in the early twenties, resulted in substantial subsidies to the private banking system which implied that the costs of running retail banks would be relatively low and therefore the probability of financial crisis relatively low. The bottom line is that the highly competitive structure of the early Federal Reserve System serves as a prototype for the design of the European Monetary Union.

To be sure, the advocates of centralization do have a point to make: competition in a monetary union need not have desirable equilibrium properties. It may lead to monetary over issue or more strikingly no equilibrium outcome whatsoever. But the circumstances generating this outcome need to be carefully specified. In particular, money must be none other than a fiat currency that can be produced *and counterfeited* at zero cost. It must be impossible (or prohibitively costly) to (1) commit to a real asset backing for your money, (2) distinguish your money from the moneys of others; that is, prevent counterfeiting, and (3) pay interest on your money.

David Glasner (1985) has argued persuasively against the impossibility of each of these conditions in a competitive setting. According to Glasner, real asset backing is an inherent feature of competitively supplied private note issue. "An endogenously determined supply of costlessly produced money can be reconciled with a finite price level under convertibility. Costless production under competitive conditions does not imply an infinite price level because competition itself compels the banks to maintain convertibility as well as to pay real interest on the cash balances they produce" (1985, pp. 63–5). How might such interest be paid?

A delicate question arises here. It is the anticipated real interest rate that is the incentive for holding the bankers' IOUs. How can this real interest be paid? Unless bankers commit themselves to convert their IOUs into an asset which they cannot create costlessly, the prospect of real interest seems illusory. There is no reason to believe a promise to pay interest unless the value of the IOU is fixed in real terms by a contractual commitment to convert either on demand or at a specified redemption date. . . . By giving holders of his IOUs the right of conversion in a real asset at a predetermined rate, a banker can guarantee them a stipulated real rate of interest. A banker may do so by establishing convertibility into a real asset expected to appreciate at a rate equal to the real rate of interest, or by announcing that the conversion rate between his IOUs and a real asset of constant value will be periodically increased in the future.   (Glasner, 1985, p. 50)

As was indicated in chapter 5, the early history of the Federal Reserve provides a somewhat different, but just as effective, solution to Glasner's "delicate question." By supplying a capital intensive in-kind payment in the form of check-clearing and currency services, holders of a reserve bank's monetary liabilities can be assured of a real rate of return. Holders can be confident that the reserve bank will not renege because they can easily observe the irreversible infrastructure that is in place to deliver the services. In countries with relatively developed financial sectors, it may be no accident that central banks supply money and financial services jointly. This is a way of surmounting the time inconsistency problem that has played such a prominent role in the recent monetary policy literature.

Finally, Glasner also has something to say about the condition (2) that a producer be able to distinguish own money from the moneys of other producers. "The violation of another money producer's trademark is not a requirement of competition, it is an infringement of property rights that we call counterfeiting" (1985, p. 49). Clearly, if this precondition does not hold, whether in a setting of note issue by private banks or a setting of note issue by reserve banks, over issue in a competitive monetary union will be a real danger.

While I have argued that the early Federal Reserve System provides an unfortunate choice for Eichengreen, there are numerous monetary case studies from which he could have drawn to illustrate his point about the pitfalls of decentralization. Consider, for instance, central banking in the republics of the former Soviet Union. The largest republic, Russia, has chosen not to commit to a real asset backing for the rouble. Also, the uncertain status of property rights in the republics means that counterfeiting is difficult to prevent and the relatively primitive nature of the financial sector means that transaction services such as check-clearing are not readily available. Taken together, these conditions make it easy for the other republics to piggyback off the printing of roubles by the Russian central bank. This case aptly illustrates the set of circumstances outlined by Rolnick and Weber: multiple central banks with each printing paper money that is indistinguishable from the others. The results, over issue and inflation, are not surprising and represent a strong confirmation of the competitive model in that they show what can go wrong when money issuers do not face a bottom-line.

9.2 Central bank independence

The historical approach taken in this book also sheds considerable light on the time-worn issue of central bank independence. For one thing, it calls into question the whole relevance of "independence" as a meaningful term in economic discourse. What does independence mean? Does it imply that decision makers are free of constraints so that they can pursue their anti-inflation preferences willy-nilly?

It should come as no surprise that I see such an interpretation as economic nonsense. Scarcity implies constraints: for you, for me, and for central bankers. Perhaps even more to the point, scarcity implies competition for limited resources. This competition is unavoidable. The only interesting question is in what forms competition will manifest itself. To say that conservative, anti-inflation central bankers naturally will take the helm of an independent central bank begs a multitude of issues. What is natural about an anti-inflation central banker? What is the appointment process that ensures a conservative will indeed be selected? What are the institutional mechanisms surrounding the operation of a central bank that ensures a conservative, if selected, will survive?

These questions boil down to the central one: What are the constraints? Admittedly, I have taken an approach in this book that may seem more than a little odd to the traditional monetary economist. In very crude form it is one which says "forget the preferences, just give me the constraints." But is this approach really so odd? After all, the price-taker assumption represents the starting point when addressing most microeconomics issues. This book simply makes the claim that "good" microeconomics is also "good" central banking economics. At the very least, working through the microeconomics of central banking should provide a sound foundation from which to evaluate issues like "what are the consequences of central bank independence?".

Contrast the microeconomics approach to independence with a "standard" approach which defends independence as a way of overcoming the problems associated with the time-inconsistency of central bank plans. An influential version of the time-inconsistency problem in monetary policy has been developed by Barro and Gordon (1983). They stress that the optimality of monetary policy depends on whether commitment is possible. One way of viewing inflation in their model is as a tax on money holdings. To induce individuals to hold money, optimal policy requires that it be taxed at a relatively low rate. Once the decision has been made by the public regarding how much to accumulate, however, money holdings can be taxed at no distortion costs. Without some sort of pre-commitment, too much inflation would be produced by the central bank.

From a modeling perspective, the easy solution is to simply assert that the central banker is able to commit; that is, to irrevocably select a level of inflation at the same time that money holders choose their money holdings. This solution has been used to justify the imposition of monetary rules on the central banker. But this ignores the possibility that technological considerations may make rules too costly to enforce.

It is in lieu of rules that some monetary economists (Rogoff, 1985) have proposed the selection of independent central bankers with preferences for inflation that are more "conservative" than those of the general population. Give conservative central bankers the freedom to do what comes naturally to them – fight inflation – and the time-inconsistency problem can be overcome.

This is a strange solution to be advocating for those sympathetic to rules. In essence, it says "give central bankers complete independence so that they can give us an inflation rate lower than what we would get with discretion." Presumably, the conservative central banker is subject to the same time-consistency problem as the generic central banker. But the solution works because the time inconsistent policy of an anti-inflation central banker results in less inflation than the time inconsistent policy of a central banker with neutral preferences. Still, something seems amiss with a solution that calls for fighting discretion with discretion.

Given the shaky underpinnings of the standard theoretical case for independence it is not surprising that empirical support is not overwhelming. Alex Cukierman provides the most comprehensive index of independence on a country-by-country basis in his book, *Central Bank Strategy, Credibility and Independence* (1992). The book uses the index to estimate the impact of independence on inflation. In reviewing *Central Bank Strategy*, Charles Goodhart (1994) observes that Cukierman "seems reasonably happy about the estimated strength of the relationships he has found between his indices and inflation." Goodhart goes on to note, however, that "This strikes me as whether you see a glass half-full or half-empty, because given all the excitement about CB independence, the empirical relationships exhibited here . . . strike me as rather weak" (1994, p. 111–12).

One problem that any empirical study must confront is the appropriate definition of independence. Is it the ability to pursue a policy that is contrary to the preferences of the rest of government? If so, then how is independence to be quantified? As Fernando Carvalho has observed, governments in industrial countries generally have the statutory power "to direct the monetary authority toward some desired behavior. Nevertheless, none of the governments studied ever used this power. Is this a sign of the moral strength of the monetary authorities deterring intervention? Or is it a sign of the central bank's compliance in matters concerning the fundamentals?" (Carvalho, 1995–6, pp. 168–9).

The microeconomics approach of this book lodges what I perceive to be an even more fundamental challenge to those monetary models which attribute price stability to the independence of a country's central bank. While one may argue that the competitive model, which has served as my basic tool of analysis, is less useful as an explanatory device during some historical episodes as compared with others, it is my contention that recent worldwide trends in information and financial technology enhance its applicability in modern monetary economies. As one important example, financial innovations which have increased the possibility of substituting among central bank moneys effectively ties the hands of any single monetary authority.

Within the context of this global competitive market for central bank money, what are we to make of the stylized fact that over the last several decades a number of developed countries have legislated central bank independence and at the same time inflation has come down? My interpretation is that a third factor is operative – competition in the central banking industry. Competition not only fosters price stability, but also tends to substitute for more "hands-on" methods that governments might use in controlling their central banks. The government need not employ expensive technologies to insure against high inflation if a competitive market provides such insurance spontaneously. The government can simply allow its central bank to run on automatic pilot. While an outside observer would tend to classify the central bank as independent in this case, and perhaps attribute price stability to this independence, at a deeper level independence could not be said to have "caused" price stability. Clearly, the driving force is competition. The whole debate about the role of independence in controlling inflation is a red herring in a worldwide competitive central banking industry.

9.3 Gold, public finance, and monetary policy in the twenty-first century

An underlying theme of this book is that Federal Reserve history has been driven by technological forces. The dominant forces have been changes in the government's financing requirements and changes in the specie backing of money. With respect to financing, the trend has been one of increasing federal government spending, punctuated by periodic wartime financing. With respect to specie backing, the trend has been a progressive, if uneven, reduction in the reserve banks' specie reserve ratio.

Gold's place in modern monetary systems has its evolutionary roots in more primitive monetary systems. Through a decentralized trial and error process, gold emerged as the dominant money in many of these primitive systems. The modern system arose when individuals started using notes backed by the issuers' commitment to convert notes into gold. This transition was made possible by a technical factor – a technological innovation which increased the cost of counterfeiting (Redish, 1993). Issuers (banks) would demonstrate their ability to convert by holding suitably large reserves of gold.

Another major step in the evolutionary process occurred in the nineteenth century with the spontaneous formation of bankers' clubs which operated as private clearinghouses. The process continued when nation-states, motivated by seigniorage concerns, either sold exclusive note-issuing rights to a privileged clearinghouse or simply nationalized the private clearinghouse system by creating a central bank. Each step in the evolutionary process was stimulated by some technical innovation, broadly defined, which served to centralize and economize the financial sector's gold reserves.

Angela Redish argues that the type of innovations responsible for the reduction in gold reserves changed in moving from the nineteenth to the twentieth century. "In the period up to 1914 economizing on gold had largely been a matter of domestic concern and the institutional innovations were at the national level. After 1914 innovations were predominantly at the international level" (Redish, 1993, p. 785).

Institutionally, innovations during the twentieth century have entailed a step-by-step relaxation of the classical gold standard constraints. The first step occurred during the inter war period. "Countries allowed the monetary authorities to hold reserves in foreign exchange and allowed them to interpret convertibility as convertibility into coin, bullion, or foreign exchange" (Redish, 1993, p. 787). Next,

Under the Bretton Woods system that actually came into effect in 1959 currencies would fix parities with the US dollar and the US dollar would be convertible into gold; that is, the US agreed to buy and sell gold at $35 an ounce. The economizing of resources had reached epic proportions. . . . The final demise of the gold link occurred in two steps: in August 1971 US President Nixon temporarily suspended the convertibility of the US dollar into gold; a suspension that became permanent in 1973.   (Redish, 1993, pp. 789, 790)

The other worldwide trend shaping the evolution of monetary institutions and outcomes in the twentieth century has been the increased financing responsibilities of nation-states. At the turn of the century revenue demands were relatively modest. For the United States, at least, significant and persistent increases in government spending did not occur until after the decade of the twenties; federal government spending permanently increased in the aftermath of the Great Depression and in the aftermath of World War II.

According to the microeconomics approach developed in this book, the evolution of the Federal Reserve System during the twentieth century can best be understood within the context of this worldwide evolutionary process. When financing requirements were modest the reserve industry was allowed to operate on automatic pilot with each of the reserve banks producing their own monetary output in a highly competitive market. This was the model of the 1920s. Later, an increase in the government's financing needs signaled an end to the competitive market structure. The story-line of the 1930s and 1940s was of a by then centralized Fed producing money alongside of another government agency, the Treasury, which also possessed money creation powers. The market contained two government money producers with each producing a money that was essentially a perfect substitute for the other's. Here, the over issue problem emphasized by modern monetary theorists was a legitimate concern. The special monetary policies which were formulated after the Great Depression and during World War II (see chapters 7 and 8) served to coordinate policy in a way that counteracted over issue.

The book also has something to say about monetary policy in the twenty-first century and how it might differ from policy in the twentieth century. In the twentieth century, monetary policy was driven largely by government financing considerations. For analytical purposes, the approach in this book follows that used by other economic historians in viewing changes in financing conditions (that is, wars) as exogenous shocks. Governments had little choice but to respond by making more intensive use of all of its revenue sources. With respect to seigniorage, this meant imposing legal restrictions on the reserve industry which tended to make it more monopolistic. In this sense, public finance caused monetary policy.

On a somewhat optimistic note, causation for the twenty-first century may be in the opposite direction. Technological innovation in the information sector has made competition an international phenomenon. Even if a national government is able to protect a domestic central bank from domestic competition, it may be unable to insulate the central bank from competition by money producers (central banks or private issuers) outside national boundaries. In this setting of worldwide competition, the opportunities for a national government to produce seigniorage are severely limited. To the extent that seigniorage is a key factor in fighting a large-scale war, competition in the central bank industry undercuts the ability of nation-states to conduct "world" wars. In contrast to the previous century, monetary economics in the twenty-first century might be said to cause, or at least define the limits of, public finance.

In this new world order, the study of monetary economics is less special but perhaps more important. Monetary economics in the twenty-first century, particularly the monetary economics of central banking, becomes less special in that the autocratic, monopoly central banking institutions that thrived in the nineteenth and twentieth centuries will have poor survival prospects in the twenty-first century. In this view, monetary economics of the twenty-first century becomes a sub-branch of microeconomics. Or put differently, there is no micro versus macro distinction; simply, *economics*. Issues like central bank independence, the personality of the central bank chair, and discretion versus rules are irrelevant in the face of binding competitive constraints. Nation-states can afford the luxury of independent structures, maverick chairs, and the appearance of discretion since monetary policy must march to the tune of the market. Of course, these market constraints are what will make the study of the *microeconomics* of central banking a paramount concern in the next century.

Notes

1 Introduction

1 See Mankiw (1987), Poterba and Rotemberg (1990), and Trehan and Walsh (1990) for recent examples of the new classical approach to money creation.

2 Microeconomics of the reserve industry

1 The economics literature offers several definitions of seigniorage. See Klein and Neumann (1990).
2 Equation (2.2) differs from Miron's formulation by allowing interest payments on reserves and reserve bank loans to banks.
3 Dowd (1994, p. 296) points to evidence that specie holding in a laissez-faire system would be small. A high degree of substitutability between reserve bank currency and specie would give this result.
4 A more extreme program insures the reserve bank against negative profits arising not only from adverse interbank clearings, but also in the course of serving as a lender of last resort to the retail system. The government agrees to underwrite any losses that reserve banks incur as a result of providing emergency lines of credit. In making this additional commitment, the government fully nationalizes the reserve bank industry.

3 Peculiar economics of the founding of the Fed

1 National bank notes were a *de facto* obligation of the Treasury. See Timberlake (1993).
2 See Toma (1982) for a general discussion of the Fed's financing structure. Goff and Toma (1993) analyze the Act's failure to authorize transfers from the government to the Fed.
3 A compulsory system of clearing replaced a voluntary one in July 1916 (see Spahr, 1926).
4 Strictly speaking, the Board would be indifferent to a market versus a penalty discount rate. With a penalty rate, $L_C = 0$. This would not be the solution chosen if the Board desired that reserve banks be actively engaged in extending discount loans.

5 At first there were a multiplicity of discount rates applying to securities of various types. The 6 percent rate is the Federal Reserve Bank of New York rate on discounts of commercial, agricultural, and livestock paper with maturities of from 31 to 60 days.

6 A temporary decrease in the interest rate would result in only a short-run earnings problem.

7 Fishe (1991) shows that the original policy was one where reserve banks backed each dollar of their monetary liabilities with 40 cents to satisfy a 40 percent gold reserve requirement. They also exercised an option of satisfying a 60 percent commercial paper collateral requirement with gold. The overall result was a 100 percent specie ratio.

8 The 1917 amendments allowed reserve banks to count towards their 40 percent gold reserve requirement any gold held to satisfy the collateral requirement (see previous note).

4 Interest on reserves and reserve smoothing in a correspondent banking system

1 Miron's work formalizes previous work (for instance, Burgess, 1936, pp. 204–6; and Friedman and Schwartz, 1963, pp. 292–3) which pointed to the Fed's influence on the pattern of interest rates. More recently, economists (see Goodfriend and King, 1988; Mankiw, Miron and Weil, 1987; and Wheelock, 1992) have used Miron's view of the founding of the Fed as the starting point for studying related issues.

2 See White (1983) for a general description of the National Bank System and Goodfriend and Hargraves (1983) for a specific account of reserve requirement regulation.

3 See Garber and Weisbrod (1992, chapter 19), Gorton (1985), Gorton and Mullineaux (1987), and Timberlake (1984) for overviews of the role of private clearinghouses before the Fed.

4 In the early 1900s, New York City banks, along with city banks in Chicago and St Louis, accounted for about 50 percent of all bankers' balances (White, 1983, p. 69).

5 See Glasner (1985) for the antecedents of this view in classical theory.

6 Following Miron, the analysis ignores reserve requirements. From 1917 to 1935 reserve requirements on Fed members were constant.

7 Equation (4.3) is based on several simplifying assumptions. For one thing, it models New York City banks as providing deposits only for country banks; in reality, they also provided deposits for the general public. Also, the equation is set up so that the city bank has a correspondent relationship with one country bank – the bank depicted by equations (4.1) and (4.2).

8 Like the country bank and city bank relationship, the city bank and clearinghouse relationship is one-on-one. That is, the loans the city bank of equation (4.3) receives equal the total loans extended by the clearinghouse. The city bank knows that for every dollar of reserves it deposits with the clearinghouse one minus the specie ratio will be returned as a loan. If the city bank were one of many banks receiving loans from a clearinghouse, then the same result would

require that the clearinghouse tie loans to each bank to the reserves of that bank.

9 Restate equation (4.9) as $c = iA$. Given that $A > 0$, a sufficient condition for c to rise with i is that the increase in i be as large as the initial value of i. Before 1914, loan rate changes of this magnitude were a characteristic feature of the autumn crop-moving season.

10 Allowing the public to hold currency issued by a clearinghouse would not change the major conclusions of the model. The primary difference is that more discount loans could be extended and larger subsidies could be distributed by the clearinghouse to the banking system.

11 Given the Miron-type cost term, $(w^2/2)[(R/BB) - 1]^2$, the city bank would set its reserve–deposit ratio at one. Any lower or higher ratio would raise costs without affecting revenues.

12 The conclusion that relaxing the legal restriction eases the financial crisis problem does not depend on the simplifying assumption that $\rho = 1$ for the private clearinghouse and $\rho = 0$ for the national clearinghouse; nor does it depend on the simplifying assumption of a zero profit constraint. Generally, a reduction in ρ increases the responsiveness of b to a change in i in competitive and monopoly settings.

13 Fishe (1991) shows that amendments to the Federal Reserve Act in 1917 significantly increased the note-issuing power of reserve banks. It is worth noting that the Fed increased its discount window and check-clearing subsidies at about the same time (see section 4.5).

14 At least some clearinghouses, however, did invest member bank deposits in highly liquid overnight loans (White, 1983, p. 75). Also, during emergencies some clearinghouses made credit available at a rate that was constant across seasons (Timberlake, 1984).

15 Although I treat k as an exogenous service cost parameter, the Fed probably is able to exercise some control over service costs. For one thing, the Fed may be able to change the quality of services provided over time.

16 The seasonal patterns for the 1922–8 period are similar to those reported for the 1917–28 period. Each seasonal pattern was constructed by first regressing the monthly values of each variable on 12 seasonal dummies (with no intercept), a trend, and trend-squared. Then, the mean value of the dummy coefficients was subtracted from each monthly dummy.

5 Competitive open market operations

1 In calculating the chiseling spread, ρ is the average specie ratio for the system, i is the call rate, and d is the highest discount rate in the System.

6 High tide of the Federal Reserve System

1 The lag lengths for the past values of securities and discounts was determined using H. Akaike's (1969) final prediction-error criterion.

2 Although table 6.2 shows the seasonal pattern to be close to statistical significance for the years 1929–33, Miron emphasizes that the standard deviation and the amplitude of the seasonal cycle in Fed credit decreased in moving from the 1920s to the 1930s.

7 The Fed, executive branch, and public Finance, 1934–1939

1 Barro's variable is the ratio of normal federal spending to GNP and can be viewed as a measure of the federal government's funding requirement from all sources of taxation and not just from money creation. The government's revenue request from the Fed is assumed to be correlated with this general requirement.

2 Unlike reserve requirements, the original Federal Reserve Act gave Congress little discretion over the scope of subsidies to the private banking system.

3 For a discussion of how this arrangement was incentive compatible see Toma (1985, pp. 372–3).

4 The decrease in reserve requirements relative to permanent government spending after World War II may be explained by the postwar rise in nominal interest rates which served to increase seigniorage for a given reserve requirement (see Toma, 1995).

5 Total federal government receipts (less transfers from the Fed) divided by nominal GNP increased from 0.055 in 1935 to 0.078 in 1937 (see Barro, 1990, table 11.1).

8 World War II financing

1 Equation (8.1) is based on the assumption that default and term premiums on private and government bonds equal zero, which is equivalent to assuming that private bonds and government bonds are perfect substitutes, as are short- and long-term bonds.

2 The minimum change in the money supply would equal the amount of bonds monetized as a result of the bill rate policy, minus the $2.2 billion of securities initially in the Fed's portfolio.

3 For (8.4), I use the annualized rate of industrial output expansion during World War II (March 1942 to March 1945) of about 8 percent as a proxy for the expected wartime real income growth rate. Based on previous studies (Barro, 1989; Toma, 1991b; Friedman and Schwartz, 1982), I also assume wartime production controls resulted in a value for u_t of between 0 and minus 10 percent and that lower and upper limits for the income elasticity of money demand are 0.5 and 1.5.

4 In Toma (1992), I show that the spread between the bill rate and rates on government coupon issues with 3 months or less to maturity generally increased during the bill program which indicates that the 3/8 percent bill rate was an administered below market rate.

References

Akaike, H. 1969. "Fitting Autoregressions for Prediction." *Annals of the Institute of Statistical Mathematics:* 243–7.

Barro, R. J. 1986. "US Deficits since World War I." *Scandinavian Journal of Economics* 88(1): 195–222.

1989. "Interest Rate Targeting." *Journal of Monetary Economics* 23: 3–30.

1990. "On the Predictability of Tax-Rate Changes." In R. J. Barro, ed., *Macroeconomic Policy*. Cambridge MA: Harvard University Press: 268–97.

1993. *Macroeconomics*. Fourth edn. New York: John Wiley & Sons, Inc.

Barro, R. J. and Gordon, D. B. 1983. "Rules, Discretion, and Reputation in a Model of Monetary Policy." *Journal of Monetary Economics* 12: 101–21.

Barsky, R. B., Mankiw, N.G., Miron, J.A., and Weil, D.N. 1988. "The Worldwide Change in the Behavior of Interest Rates in 1915." *European Economic Review* 32: 1123–47.

Board of Governors of the Federal Reserve System. 1943. *Banking and Monetary Statistics*. Washington DC.

Board of Governors of the Federal Reserve System. 1945. *Annual Report*. Washington DC.

1976. *Banking and Monetary Statistics*. Washington DC.

Bordo, M. and Kydland, F. E. 1992. "The Gold Standard as a Rule." Federal Reserve Bank of Cleveland, *Working Paper* (March).

Buchanan, J. M. and Tullock, G. 1962. *The Calculus of Consent*. Ann Arbor: The University of Michigan Press.

Burgess, W. R. 1936. *The Reserve Banks and the Money Market*. Revised edn. New York: Harper and Brothers.

Carvalho, F. 1995–6. "The Independence of Central Banks: A Critical Assessment of the Arguments." *Journal of Post Keynesian Economics* 18: 159–75.

Chandler, L.V. 1958. *Benjamin Strong, Central Banker*. Washington: Brookings Institution.

Clark, T. A. 1986. "Interest Rate Seasonals and the Federal Reserve." *Journal of Political Economy* 94 (February): 76–125.

Conway, T. 1914. "The Financial Policy of the Federal Reserve Banks." *Journal of Political Economy* 22(4): 319–31.

Cover, J. P. and Schutte, D. P. 1990. "The Stability of Money-Supply Policies that Peg the Interest Rate." *Southern Economic Journal* (October): 330–9.

Crawford, A. 1972. *Monetary Management under the New Deal*. New York: De Capa Press.

Cukierman, A. 1992. *Central Bank Strategy, Credibility and Independence*. Cambridge, MA: MIT Press.

D'Arista, J. W. 1994. *The Evolution of US Finance*, Volume I. London: M.E. Sharpe.

Dowd, K. 1994. "Competitive Banking, Bankers' Clubs, and Bank Regulation." *Journal of Money, Credit, and Banking* 26(2): 289–308.

Duprey, J. N. and Nelson, C. W. 1986. "A Visible Hand: The Fed's Involvement in the Check Payments System." Federal Reserve Bank of Minneapolis, *Quarterly Review* 10(2): 18–29.

Eichengreen, B. 1992. "How Ben Strong Would Have Done It." *The International Economy* (March/April): 36–8.

Eichengreen, B. and Garber, P. 1991. "Before the Accord: US Monetary-Financial Policy, 1945–51." In Glenn Hubbard, ed., *Financial Markets and Financial Crises*. Chicago: University of Chicago Press: 175–206.

Fishe, R. 1991. "The Federal Reserve Amendments of 1917: The Beginning of a Seasonal Note Issue." *Journal of Money, Credit, and Banking* 23(3) Pt. 1: 308–26.

Friedman, M. 1959. *A Program for Monetary Stability*. New York: Fordham University Press.

Friedman, M. and Schwartz, A. J. 1963. *A Monetary History of the United States, 1867–1960*. Princeton: Princeton University Press.

    1982. *Monetary Trends in the United States and the United Kingdom*. Chicago: University of Chicago Press.

Garber, P. M. and Weisbrod, S. 1992. *The Economics of Banking, Liquidity, and Money*. Lexington MA: D. C. Heath.

Giannini, C. 1995. "Money, Trust, and Central Banking." *Journal of Economics and Business* 47: 217–37.

Glasner, D. 1985. "A Reinterpretation of Classical Monetary Theory." *Southern Economic Journal* 52(1): 46–67.

Goff, B. and Toma, M. 1993. "Optimal Seigniorage, the Gold Standard, and Central Bank Financing." *Journal of Money, Credit, and Banking* 25(1): 79–95.

Goodfriend, M. and Hargraves, M. 1983. "A Historical Assessment of the Rationales and Functions of Reserve Requirements." Federal Reserve Bank of Richmond, *Economic Review* (March).

Goodfriend, M. and King, R. 1988. "Financial Deregulation, Monetary Policy, and Central Banking." Federal Reserve Bank of Richmond, *Economic Review* (May/June): 3–21.

Goodhart, C. 1987. "Why Do Banks Need a Central Bank?" *Oxford Economic Papers* 39: 75–89.

    1988. *The Evolution of Central Banks*. Cambridge MA and London: MIT Press.

Gorton, G. 1985. "Clearinghouses and the Origin of Central Banking in the United States." *Journal of Economic History* 45 (June): 277–83.

Gorton, G. and Mullineaux, D. 1987. "The Joint Production of Confidence: Endogenous Regulation and Nineteenth-Century Commercial Bank Clearing-houses." *Journal of Money, Credit, and Banking* 19 (November): 457–68.

Grossman, H. 1990. "The Political Economy of War Debt and Inflation." In William Haraf and Phillip Cagan, eds., *Monetary Policy for a Changing Financial Environment* (Washington DC): 166–81.

Holland, S. A. and Toma, M. 1991. "The Role of the Federal Reserve as 'Lender of Last Resort' and the Seasonal Fluctuation of Interest Rates." *Journal of Money, Credit, and Banking* 23(4): 659–76.

Kareken, J. H. and Wallace, N. 1981. "On the Indeterminacy of Equilibrium Exchange Rates." *Quarterly Journal of Economics* 96(2): 207–22.

King, R., Wallace, N., and Weber, W. 1992. "Nonfundamental Uncertainty and Exchange Rates." *Journal of International Economics* 32 (February): 83–108.

Klein, M. and Neumann, M. 1990. "Seigniorage: What is It and Who Gets It?" *Weltwirtschaftliches Archiv* 2: 205–21.

Mankiw, N. G. 1987. "The Optimal Collection of Seigniorage, Theory and Evidence." *Journal of Monetary Economics* 20: 327–41.

Mankiw, N. G., Miron, J. A., and Weil, D. N. 1987. "The Adjustment of Expectations to a Change in Regime: A Study of the Founding of the Federal Reserve." *American Economic Review:* 358–74.

Miron, J. A. 1986. "Financial Panics, the Seasonality of the Nominal Interest Rate, and the Founding of the Fed." *American Economic Review* 76: 125–40.

Murphy, H. 1950. *The National Debt in War and Transition.* New York.

Plosser, C. I. 1990. "Money and Business Cycles: A Real Cycle Interpretation." In Michael Belongia, ed., *Monetary Policy on the Fed's 75th Anniversary.* Proceedings of the 14th Annual Economic Policy Conference of the Federal Reserve Bank of St. Louis. Norwell MA: Kluwer Academic Publishers.

Poterba, J. M. and Rotemberg, J. J. 1990. "Inflation and Taxation with Optimizing Governments." *Journal of Money, Credit, and Banking* 22: 1–18.

Redish, A. 1993. "Anchors Aweigh: The Transition from Commodity Money to Fiat Money in Western Economies." *Canadian Journal of Economics* 26(4): 777–95.

Rockoff, H. 1984. *Drastic Measures: A History of Wage and Price Controls in the States.* New York.

Rogoff, K. 1985. "The Optimal Degree of Commitment to an Intermediate Monetary Target." *Quarterly Journal of Economics* 100: 1169–90.

Rolnick, A. J. and Weber, W. 1989. "A Case for Fixing Exchange Rates." Federal Reserve Bank of Minneapolis, *Annual Report:* 3–14.

Rolnick, A. J., Smith, B., and Weber, W. 1993. "In Order to Form a More Perfect Monetary Union." Federal Reserve Bank of Minneapolis, *Quarterly Review* (Fall): 2–13.

1994. "Establishing a Monetary Union: The United States Experience." *1995 American Social Science Association Abstracts* 9(3): 20–2.

Selgin, G. A. and White, L. H. 1987. "The Evolution of a Free Banking System." *Economic Inquiry* 25: 439–58.

1994. "Monetary Reform and the Redemption of National Bank Notes, 1863–1913." *Business History Review* 68: 205–43.

Smith, J. G. 1932. "The Concentration of Funds and Transactions in the New York Money Market with Special Reference to Bankers' Balances." In B. H.

Beckhart and J. G. Smith, eds., *The New York Money Market*, Volume II. New York: Columbia University Press.

Spahr, W. E. 1926. *The Clearing and Collection of Checks*. New York: The Bankers Publishing Co.

Sprague, O.M.W. 1910. *History of Crises under the National Banking System*. Report by the National Monetary Commission to the US Senate 61st Cong., 2nd session, S. Doc. 538. Washington DC.

1913. *Banking Reform in the United States*. Cambridge MA: Harvard University Press.

Taylor, F. M. 1914. "The Elasticity of Note Issue Under the New Currency Law." *Journal of Political Economy* 22(4): 453–63.

Timberlake, R. H. 1978. *The Origins of Central Banking in the United States*. Cambridge MA: Harvard University Press.

1984. "The Central Banking Role of Clearing House Associations." *Journal of Money, Credit, and Banking* 16: 1–15.

1993. *Monetary Policy in the United States*. Chicago: University of Chicago Press.

Toma, M. 1982. "Inflationary Bias of the Federal Reserve System: A Bureaucratic Perspective." *Journal of Monetary Economics* 10: 163–90.

1985. "A Duopoly Theory of Government Money Production: The 1930s and 1940s." *Journal of Monetary Economics* 15: 363–82.

1989. "Policy Effectiveness of Open Market Operations in the 1920s." *Explorations in Economic History* 26: 99–116.

1991a. "The Demise of the Public-interest Model of the Federal Reserve System." *Journal of Monetary Economics* 27: 157–63.

1991b. "World War II, Interest Rates and Fiscal Policy Commitments." *Journal of Macroeconomics* (Summer): 459–77.

1992. "Interest Rate Controls: The United States in the 1940s." *The Journal of Economic History* 52(3): 631–50.

1995. "A Positive Theory of Reserve Requirements and Interest on Reserves." *Working Paper*.

Trehan, B. and Walsh, C.E. 1990. "Seigniorage and Tax Smoothing in the United States: 1914–1986." *Journal of Monetary Economics* 25: 97–112.

West, R. C. 1977. *Banking Reform and the Federal Reserve 1863–1923*. Ithaca: Cornell University Press.

Wheelock, D. 1991. *The Strategy and Consistency of Federal Reserve Policy, 1924–1933*. Cambridge: Cambridge University Press.

1992. "Seasonal Accommodation and the Financial Crises of the Great Depression: Did the Fed 'Furnish an Elastic Currency'?" Federal Reserve Bank of St. Louis, *Review* 74(6): 3–18.

White, E. N. 1983. *The Regulation and Reform of the American Banking System, 1900–1929*. Princeton: Princeton University Press.

Willis, H. P. 1923. *The Federal Reserve System*. New York: The Ronald Press Company.

Index